# UNDERSTANDING
## THE SEVEN CHURCHES
# OF REVELATION

D1158535

DR. JONATHAN WELTON

Welton Academy
P.O. Box 92126
Rochester, NY 14692
http://www.weltonacademy.com

ISBN 978-0-9905752-4-5

Printed in the United States of America

# DEDICATION

The seven letters of Revelation 2–3 are some of the most abused and misused passages in the entire New Testament. It is with this in mind that I dedicate this work to the Body of Christ on the earth today. It is my hope that those who have hammered others about the "Jezebel Spirit" or about being "lukewarm" or claiming that we are the living in the "Laodicean age" will finally be silenced by the facts and set free by the truth.

My greatest thanks belongs to two archeologists, Gurkan Adali and Dr. Mark Wilson. Your ongoing efforts are making such an important difference. Thank you.

# CONTENTS

# INTRODUCTION

Revelation has always fascinated me. As a theologically curious seventeen-year-old, I read every Watchman Nee book I could get my hands on. Of them all, the one that most captivated my imagination was *The Orthodoxy of the Church*, a ninety-page work on the seven churches in Revelation 2–3. Yet when I reached the end, I felt stunned and disappointed, because I had wanted to understand what was going on with those historical churches in the first century, and Nee had not told me.

For the most part, those from a dispensational background, like Watchman Nee, spiritualize the seven letters into seven time periods of Church history without looking at the historical context. And those who are not dispensationalists typically ignore them. The reason so many people have overlooked these letters is, at least in part, because they do not think they are relevant to us.

In the years since my disappointment with Nee's book, I have read other more historically thorough sources, and I have done my own research, including traveling to and touring the modern locations of each of these seven churches. In doing so, I've discovered an incredible list of connections between the cultural, geographical, and historical events of the first century in these cities and the contents of Jesus' letters to them.

Now, many years later, I've written the book I wish I had read when I was seventeen and eager to understand what these beautiful yet cryptic letters were all about. Many commentaries on the Book of Revelation give the seven letters little to no coverage. Here, I am attempting to correct that oversight by making them the center of conversation. Though many have seen them as periphery, I believe these letters hold significant and relevant information that influences our understanding of the Book of Revelation as a whole and that holds practical relevance for our lives. I hope and believe that what I share here will make these often misunderstood letters clear in the light of history.

# one

# A PROPER METHODOLOGY

When we think of Revelation, we tend to think of John's vision of Heaven and the action scenes that follow. We think of the seals, trumpets, and bowls. We debate the meaning of these passages—literal or figurative, past or future. But not many of us stop to truly consider the seven letters that begin the Book of Revelation. In fact, many commentaries give them only brief coverage before moving on to the more "exciting" material of later chapters. However, a full understanding of the Book of Revelation must begin with chapters 1–3. "The Apocalypse is a work of art, marvelous art, divine art."[1] We must examine it in its whole, as we would a fine painting. We must not leave any parts out, as each holds a clue to the overarching theme. For that reason, in this book we will examine in depth the seven letters contained in Revelation 2–3.

---

[1] Hendriksen, 59. I take this same approach to Revelation as art in my book, *The Art of Revelation*, in which I examine Revelation 4–22 as if I was an art expert explaining a masterpiece to an art novice.

Before we begin to look at the individual letters, we must first find a proper approach in our study, what some would call our methodology or hermeneutic.

## THE DISPENSATIONAL SLANT

What little has been written about the seven letters in Revelation tends to utilize a lens of interpretation called dispensationalism. This is the perspective Nee used in the book that so fascinated me as a teenager—*The Orthodoxy of the Church*. Dispensationalism teaches that Revelation 2–3 is a spiritualized explanation of seven time periods in Church history, known as dispensations. Accordingly, Nee lined up the seven churches with seven time periods throughout history, arguing that each of the early churches represented a spiritual climate in Church history. So, for example, Ephesus represents the early Church, Sardis represents the Reformation, and Laodicea represents the modern Church.[2]

Many well-known theologians have easily and thoroughly debunked the error of dispensationalism. In *More Than Conquerors*, Hendriksen says of it:

> The notion that these seven churches describe seven successive periods of Church history hardly needs refutation. To say nothing about the almost humorous— if it were not so deplorable—exegesis which, for example, makes the church at Sardis, which was dead, refer to

---

[2] Dispensationalism originated in the 1830s, so it is still a new concept in the history of the Church. Thus, it may seem to make sense that the Laodicean age could apply from the 1830s till the present. But the longer history progresses, the harder it will be to accept this view.

the glorious age of the Reformation; it should be clear to every student of the Bible that there is not one atom of evidence in all the sacred writings which in any way corroborates this thoroughly arbitrary way of cutting up the history of the Church and assigning the resulting pieces to the respective epistles of Revelation 2 and 3.[3]

The primary problem with dispensationalism, as Hendriksen points out, is that the Bible gives no proof or reason for arriving at the conclusions of dispensationalism. This system of interpretation is derived completely apart from the Scripture.

Revelation gives us no indication that the letters to the churches are anything but letters to churches in the first century. Church history tells us that each of these churches was a literal historical church (not a metaphor) and that John was addressing specific situations relevant to each church during the first century. In other words, these letters to the seven churches are clearly and deeply rooted in a historical context. When we look at the historical and cultural dynamics of the cities, we find that the letters are in fact very specific and unique to the historical reality. This would not have been necessary if these letters were metaphorical. The truth is, as we will soon see in much greater detail, John was scribing these letters from Jesus to each of these churches in context to encourage and assist them in their specific circumstances.

Further, if Jesus was using the letters to the churches as a prophetic picture (as dispensationalism claims), we would expect some sort of clue to that in the picture. For example, in Daniel 4, King Nebuchadnezzar has a dream in which he sees

---

[3] Hendriksen, 60.

a statue that has a golden head, a silver chest, bronze legs, and feet of iron and clay. Daniel interprets this figure to represent different kingdoms and time periods. Later, in Daniel 7, Daniel has a dream involving four beasts, and each of these beasts represents particular kingdoms and time periods. These two prophetic images are similar to what the dispensationalists try to find in Revelation 2–3. They each contain a picture that points to different time periods.

However, Revelation 2–3 contains no evidence that this passage is like the dreams in Daniel. It does not include mysterious symbols (like a statue of varying metals or fantastical beasts). It also does not include a clear method of interpretation. In his book, Daniel interpreted these symbolic dreams for the reader, making it clear what the symbols meant. But John did not do that. He infers no symbols because, in fact, he was not writing symbolically. He was writing to literal people, some of whom he would have personally known (we know he at least had relationships within the church at Ephesus). If God was trying to communicate about mysterious dispensations represented by these seven churches, He should have been clearer—since nobody understood these churches as mythical dispensations until the 1800s. Because He was clear about it in Daniel 4 and 7, we have every reason to believe He would have been clear about it in Revelation, too, if that was what He intended. The absolute lack of any indication that these letters are symbolic must lead us to conclude that they are literal and that dispensationalism's interpretation is completely misguided.

To this evidence against dispensationalism, David Chilton adds the further matter of logic and timing:

Does it make sense that Christ would promise the church in Philadelphia protection from something that would happen thousands of years later? "Be of good cheer, you faithful, suffering Christians of the first-century Asia Minor: I won't let those Soviet missiles and Killer Bees of the 20th century get you!" When the Philadelphian Christians were worried about more practical, immediate concerns—official persecution, religious discrimination, social ostracism, and economic boycotts—what did they care about Hal Lindsey's lucrative horror stories?[4]

It simply does not make sense. Instead, it is what Milton Terry, nineteenth-century author of the classic, *Biblical Hermeneutics*, calls "the fiction of extremists."[5]

## THE HISTORICAL-CONTEXTUAL METHOD

The better way to approach Scripture is the historical-contextual method. This is the approach we will use to understand the seven letters of Revelation. People sometimes ask why we need a methodology or hermeneutic. "Why can't we just read it?" they wonder. The answer is simple. If a person wrote a letter to a dear friend, that friend would not need a method of interpretation to understand the letter, because it was written with him in mind. It was written between two people alive at the same time in the same culture, speaking the same language, and familiar with the same idioms and terminology.

We are used to the way we talk and the slang and figures of speech we use, but people outside our specific culture and time

---

[4] Chilton, 129.
[5] Terry, 313.

period will have difficulty understanding much of what we say, even if they also speak English. Anyone who has tried to teach English as a second language or to communicate with English speakers from another culture will testify to how frequently we use figures of speech and how nonsensical and misguiding these figures of speech can be to those from a different culture. If this is true between people living at the same time, it is even truer when it comes to understanding ancient literature.

For example, consider the *Epic of Gilgamesh*, Babylonian literature from over four thousand years ago. If a group of modern people all read the *Epic of Gilgamesh* and then got together for a book discussion, each person would have a different interpretation. The meaning would not be obvious, because we do not understand the culture, language, context, and history of the piece. So, in the book discussion, people might go around the circle and say what the text *means to them*. But that is not the point. What it means to a modern reader is not relevant, because it was not written to a modern reader. It was written for ancient Babylonians. The idea that we can personally interpret ancient literature devalues the original work and author.

If I wrote a letter to my wife, and several thousand years from now people found that letter and tried to understand what I wrote, they should not make the letter mean something I never intended. If they did, they would be twisting my words, making my letter say what they wanted it to say, not what it actually meant between my wife and me. Unfortunately, this is often how people approach Scripture. What a passage might mean to an individual is not important. What matters is what the passage meant when it was written—what the Holy Spirit intended to say. This is the true meaning. Yes, God can and does speak to us with personal application through the Scripture, but this personal application must always follow a correct historical-contextual understanding.

When we read Revelation 2–3, we are reading someone else's mail. Like the letters written to Timothy, Titus, and Philemon, the letters of Revelation say they are written to a particular audience (an audience that does not include us). Jesus told John, *"Write on a scroll what you see and send it to the seven churches..."* (Rev 1:11). We are reading letters that were not written to us and that were written two thousand years ago, in a different era and culture. We don't know John personally, and we don't live in the same period of history. Because of this, at times the content of these letters is very isolated, very unique to that particular group and time. For example, no modern group known as the Nicolaitans exists, and even in history, very little is known about them.

Therefore, we need the historical-contextual method of interpretation to help us understand the framework and experience the original readers had when they read their letters. This method helps us, as much as is possible, to put ourselves in the shoes of the biblical writers and the first century audience. The theologian Gordon Fee has said, "A text cannot mean what it never meant."[6] This is absolutely vital for us to remember as we interpret the Bible and especially the Book of Revelation. For example, when Revelation 12:14 mentions the wings of a great eagle, modern readers should not interpret this to be about the United States of America (because of our national bird), because John had no knowledge of the USA. Yet some people have actually interpreted it this way. That is the embarrassing state of modern pastoral hermeneutics!

---

[6] Fee and Stuart, *How to Read the Bible for All It's Worth*, 30.

This is proof that when we lack a proper methodology, we can make anything mean anything. We can twist and manipulate and misunderstand—and that is not what we want to do. As students of the Word, we want to understand it in its proper location and according to its original intent. This is just what the historical-contextual method enables us to do. Instead of interpreting based on our modern understanding and symbolism, if we want to arrive at the correct understanding of these letters, we must restrict ourselves to what John, as the author, would have known and had access to. As we do this, we will discover that this methodology leads us to solid answers and profound understanding of the seven letters of Revelation.

In this, the historical-contextual method is a gift to us, because it gives us a window into the world of the New Testament, the world prior to AD 70. Though our modern world is so far in time and culture from that of the Bible, through historical writings and archeological findings, we can piece together the clues needed for a more accurate understanding of what the Bible really means. We begin to see what life was really like for the first century Christians—and some of the unique trials they faced. We meet characters like the Judiazers and Nicolatians, whom we have no modern context for, and through seeing them historically, we can learn not to repeat their errors in doctrine.

In the Revelation letters, as well as the letters of the remainder of the New Testament, we get snapshots of the Church prior to AD 70. Of course, these Revelation letters are special, because they do not just contain John's human side of the story. They contain Jesus' divine commentary. Also, they provide an update since the writings of Paul, who had died several years before these letters were written. Because Revelation was written just a few years before AD 70, it gives us the most current picture of what it was like for the Christians leading up to this all-important event. When we realize this, we begin to see that the historical and cultural context give a great gift to us—the gift of understanding.

Toward that end, in the next chapter, we will employ the historical-contextual method to see *who* John was writing to, *where* John was writing, *when* John was writing, *what* John was writing about, and *why* John was writing.

# UNDERSTANDING THE CONTEXT

# two

The historical-contextual method begins with the questions *who, where, when, what,* and *why.* These questions help us play the detective with the Revelation letters in order to understand, as much as possible, what was really going on when John wrote them. In this chapter, we will answer these questions in an overarching manner, as they relate to the letters as a group and to the Book of Revelation as a whole. In later chapters, we will delve more deeply into the historical context of each individual letter.

## WHO?

The first question is: *who* wrote the letter, and *who* received the letter? The apostle John wrote the Book of Revelation while exiled on the Isle of Patmos.

*I, John, your brother and companion in the suffering and kingdom and patient endurance that are ours in Jesus, was on the island of Patmos because of the word of God and the testimony of Jesus* (Revelation 1:9).

While John was on Patmos, Jesus appeared to him and gave him seven messages for seven literal and historic churches in first century Asia Minor, which is modern day Turkey.

## WHERE?

The second question is *where* was John, and *where* was he writing to? John had been imprisoned on the Island of Patmos, a small island in the Mediterranean Sea (or "Great Sea") about sixty miles off the coast of Turkey. Greece is northwest of Patmos, and Turkey is east. Israel is southeast.

John had been exiled from the mainland to this little island, and there he wrote these letters to seven churches on the mainland. Later in his life, John returned to the mainland and lived out the remainder of his days in Ephesus. The cities that John wrote to were cities in Turkey along a major Roman road. The nearest port city was Ephesus. From there, the road went to Smyrna, then Pergamum (The Roman headquarters for Asia Minor), then Thyatira, then Sardis, then Philadelphia, and finally Laodicea. This is the order of the letters he wrote, and it's the order in which a courier would have delivered them. Scholars believe the order of the cities in the seven letters follows an ancient postal route.[7]

---

[7] Ramsay, 134; Cimok, 21.

# WHEN?

The third question is, *when* was this written? In this case, the answer is complicated. While the text clearly states *who* and *where*, it does not tell us *when*. And the dating of this letter has been fiercely debated among theologians. The reason *when* matters is because it helps us understand the *what* and *why* of the letter. Whether Revelation was written before or after one of the biggest events in Jewish history—the AD 70 destruction of Jerusalem—makes a significant difference in how we understand its purpose and meaning.

Those who believe Revelation was written about future endtime events tend to hold to a later dating, after AD 70. This dating is based almost entirely on a quote from the Church father, Irenaeus. Writing in AD 180, Irenaeus said, "For it was seen not very long time since, but almost in our day, towards the end of Domitian's reign."[8] This seems to indicate that the apostle John wrote Revelation during the reign of Domitian in AD 96.

However, Kenneth Gentry (and others) have pointed out that this quote is unclear and has possibly been mistranslated. The usual translation of the pronoun is "it," but the original language is ambiguous about what the pronoun refers back to (the vision, the written book, or the apostle John). In other words, it could just as easily be translated, "For he [John] was seen not very long time since...."[9] Since John lived till nearly AD 100, this could be a very reasonable translation. And considering the other evidence in favor of an earlier dating of the Book of Revelation, it seems to also be the more logical translation.

---

[8] *Adversus haereses* 5, 30, 3.
[9] Gentry, *Before Jerusalem Fell*, 46–48.

Without this one ambiguous sentence from Irenaeus, all the evidence from within John's writing itself clearly points to a date of writing prior to the destruction of Jerusalem in AD 70.

Even if we accept Irenaeus' statement as it is typically translated, it is not conclusive evidence in favor of a later dating since Domitian also ruled Rome during AD 70. After the death of Nero, the Roman Empire experienced a lot of chaos and upheaval, including the rapid succession of multiple emperors. Domitian was one of those rulers, and he sat on the throne for nine months during the year AD 70.[10] This means Irenaeus' statement could point to a date just prior to the destruction of Jerusalem.

Compared to the evidence for a later date, the evidence that supports a pre–AD 70 dating of Revelation is abundant.[11] We will only touch briefly on a few of the evidences here. First, it is logical to assume that if a traumatic event like the destruction of Jerusalem and the Temple system had happened prior to the writing of the New Testament, that event would have been mentioned in some way. It affected Jewish life and religion from top to bottom in very significant ways. Yet it is not mentioned or alluded to as a past event at all in the New Testament. It is very difficult to believe that, had Revelation been written after AD 70, John would not have mentioned the destruction of Jerusalem and the Temple, especially since both Jerusalem and the Temple are featured in the book.

---

[10] Viola, 171–172. This is also confirmed in Wilson, *Revelation*, 5.

[11] In his book, *Re-dating the New Testament*, John A.T. Robinson gives conclusive proof that every book of the New Testament was written before the destruction of Jerusalem in AD 70.

Second, the earliest manuscript, called the *Syriac Peshitta*, has this statement at the beginning of the Book of Revelation: *"Again, the Revelation, which was upon John, the Holy Evangelist from God, when he was on the island of Patmos where he was thrown by the Emperor Nero."* This clearly indicates that the book was written during the reign of Nero, in AD 54–68.

Third, the internal evidence in the seven letters of Revelation clearly points to a pre–AD 70 writing. For example, Revelation 2:9 and 3:9 refer to the *"synagogue of Satan"* and the Jewish persecution of the Church in both Smyrna and Philadelphia. This persecution of Christians by Jews was specific to the time period prior to AD 70. In AD 70, in response to the Jewish revolt against the Roman Empire, Rome sent Titus to Jerusalem, where he decimated the city and slaughtered 1.1 million Jews.[12] And on his way to and from Jerusalem, he slaughtered as many Jews as he could all across the Roman Empire. In total, millions of Jews died, and after AD 70, they were never again in a position to persecute Christians. Thus, these references to the synagogue of Satan only make sense if the book was written before AD 70.

Fourth, John wrote his letters with incredible urgency about what was soon going to overtake these churches. Four times in the first three chapters he emphasizes the nearness of the prophesied Great Tribulation:

- What must *shortly* take place (see Rev. 1:1)

---

[12] Eusebius, in *The Church History*, 3.5, says: "I must, however, point out how Josephus estimates that the people from all over Judea, who at the time of the Passover thronged into Jerusalem as if into a prison and they numbered three million." In other words, the population of Jerusalem had more than doubled due to the Passover, so the number of Jews killed in AD 70 was probably closer to 3 million.

- For the time is *near* (see Rev. 1:3)

- I am coming to you *quickly* (see Rev. 2:16)

- I am coming *quickly* (see Rev. 3:11)

If John wrote this toward the beginning of Nero's reign, then it makes perfect sense, because in the very near future, the Roman Empire would launch a terrible persecution of the Christians in AD 64–68. And shortly after that, the Roman Army would come through Asia Minor, killing Jews on their way to destroy Jerusalem. This was a matter of great urgency for John and the churches at that time.

However, if John was writing in AD 96, it would not have made sense for John to warn the churches of coming persecution. At that point, the Church had been persecuted for several decades, and under Domitian they experienced only minor persecution compared that what they had faced under Nero in the years leading up to AD 70. Though some people believe Domitian severely persecuted the Church, archeologists refer to this as "the Domitian myth," because they have found no evidence of Domitian persecuting the Church.[13] The only way to logically explain John's warning of persecution, if Revelation was written in AD 96, is to push that persecution off to a far distant time. This is what those who believe in a future Great Tribulation do. Yet this completely overlooks the urgency and time sensitivity of John's letters. The most sensible and accurate explanation is, instead, that John wrote during the Jewish persecution of the early Church just prior to the destruction of Jerusalem.[14]

---

[13] Wilson, *Revelation*, 4.

[14] For more proof for any early dating of the Book of Revelation, see my other book, *The Art of Revelation*.

# WHAT?

The fourth question we must ask about the seven letters is *what*? What was John's purpose and subject in writing? These seven letters are different from the other letters in Scripture. In modern terms, we could compare them to postcards. They are brief and to the point, and they are open letters in a single document that was passed between the seven churches. So, as Gordon Fee says, "All the believers who are to receive this document end up reading everyone else's mail, as it were."[15] This is unique to the Book of Revelation. The other pastoral epistles in the New Testament were addressed to a single group or region, not multiple regions, as we see here.

Yet even though they are addressed to different churches, common themes of commendation, rebuke, and promise are woven throughout the letters. According to N.T. Wright, this means that though the letters were specific to the seven churches, at the same time, the promises and warnings were without borders:

> We should not imagine that Christians in Ephesus *only* are promised the right to eat from the tree of life, or that those in Smyrna *only* are promised that they will escape the second death, and so on. All the promises, all the warnings, are for all the churches.[16]

This overlap is precisely because the overarching message of the letters is the same. Each points to the coming Roman persecution and the destruction of Jerusalem, not in hopes of preventing them but in order to warn and encourage the

---

[15] Fee, *Revelation*, 22.
[16] Wright, 12.

believers in the face of them. John wrote to provide a framework through which these believers could understand the horrible events that were about to happen.

This is declared in the very first sentence of the book: *"The revelation of Jesus Christ, which God gave him to show to his servants the things that must soon take place..."* (Rev. 1:1 ESV). In Greek, the word translated as "revelation" is *apokalupsis*, which means "an uncovering or unveiling."[17] This declaration that John intends to reveal or unveil Jesus should cause us to ask what was veiling Him or hiding Him in the first place. We will discuss this in the next chapter. For here, what's important to understand is that John's *what* was the unveiling or revelation of Jesus and the changes about to come on the earth.

## WHY?

The fifth and final question is *why?* Why did John write these letters and the Book of Revelation? Obviously, the content—the *what*—of the message is part of it. But it goes beyond that. In his declaration of the coming destruction of Jerusalem, John intentionally wrote Revelation in a very particular style and to a particular audience. Knowing why he did this is essential to our understanding of the seven letters.

## PARALLELS TO THE OLD TESTAMENT PROPHETS

First, John wrote Revelation as a parallel to the writings of Ezekiel, Jeremiah, and Isaiah, who prophesied the destruction of Jerusalem by the Babylonians in 586 BC. Ezekiel, Jeremiah, and

---

[17] *Strong's Concordance*, Greek #602.

Isaiah are the most directly quoted books in Revelation, and the similarities between them and Revelation is startling. Ezekiel, in particular, was in John's mind as he wrote. The parallels in imagery and language are undeniable:

1.  The Throne Vision (Rev. 4; Ezek. 1)

2.  The Book (Rev. 5; Ezek. 2–3)

3.  The Four Plagues (Rev. 6:1–8; Ezek. 5)

4.  The Slain under the Altar (Rev. 6:9–11; Ezek. 6)

5.  The Wrath of God (Rev. 6:12–17; Ezek. 7)

6.  The Seal on the Saint's Foreheads (Rev. 7; Ezek. 9)

7.  The Coals from the Altar (Rev. 8; Ezek. 10)

8.  No More Delay (Rev. 10:1–7; Ezek. 12)

9.  The Eating of the Book (Rev. 10:8–11; Ezek. 2)

10. The Measuring of the Temple (Rev. 11:1–2; Ezek. 40–43)

11. Jerusalem and Sodom (Rev. 11:8; Ezek. 16)

12. The Cup of Wrath (Rev. 14; Ezek. 23)

13. The Vine of the Land (Rev. 14:18–20; Ezek. 15)

14. The Great Harlot (Rev. 17–18; Ezek. 16, 23)

15. The Lament over the City (Rev. 18; Ezek. 27)

16. The Scavengers' Feast (Rev. 19; Ezek. 39)

17. The First Resurrection (Rev. 20:4–6; Ezek. 37)

18. The Battle with Gog and Magog (Rev. 20:7–9; Ezek. 38–39)

19. The New Jerusalem (Rev. 21; Ezek. 40–48)

20. The River of Life (Rev. 22; Ezek. 47)

Many modern Christians miss these parallels simply because they are not well-versed in the Old Testament. However, the Jews and Christians of John's day would have known exactly what he was doing. They would have seen that by paralleling these Old Testament prophets, John was declaring another destruction of Jerusalem. In the same way that Babylon had come, so too Rome would come and destroy Jerusalem and the Temple. History tells us that not only did the destruction happen in AD 70, but it happened on the exact same day of the calendar year as the destruction of 586 BC—on the ninth of Av.

However, the story comes with a twist, because in the Old Testament, Babylon was the enemy who came and destroyed Jerusalem. But in the New Testament, Jerusalem has become like Babylon in God's eyes, and God comes to destroy Jerusalem. This is the picture John painted in Revelation, and because he used Old Testament imagery and language, his readers knew exactly what he was prophesying.

## PARALLELS TO THE SYNOPTIC GOSPELS

Second, John also wrote Revelation to directly parallel some of the content of the synoptic gospels. Matthew, Mark, and Luke have a lot of parallels. They are like three eye-witness accounts of the same story in ways that may differ a little but are mostly the same. By comparison, John's gospel is very different from the others, and it leaves out some important material that the others all have. So part of John's *why* is the filling in of some gaps left by his gospel. One of the items John left out was the Olivet Discourse (see Matt. 24; Mark 13; Luke 21), which predicted the destruction of Jerusalem. So, in Revelation we get John's version of the Olivet Discourse, only on a much grander scale, because he expands it to parallel the symbolism of Ezekiel.

When it comes to the seven letters to the churches in Revelation 2–3, we also find some very interesting parallels to the synoptic gospels, particularly in the use of several repetitive statements from Jesus. The first of these statements is: *"Whoever has ears, let them hear."* This phrase occurs seven times in the synoptic gospels (see Matt. 11:15; 13:9, 43; Mark 4:9, 23; Luke 8:8; Luke 14:35).

---

*Whoever has ears, let them hear* (Matthew 11:15).

*Whoever has ears, let them hear* (Matthew 13:9).

*Then the righteous will shine like the sun in the kingdom of their Father. Whoever has ears, let them hear* (Matthew 13:43).

*Then Jesus said, "Whoever has ears to hear, let them hear"* (Mark 4:9)

*If anyone has ears to hear, let them hear* (Mark 4:23).

*Still other seed fell on good soil. It came up and yielded a crop, a hundred times more than was sown." When he said this, he called out, "Whoever has ears to hear, let them hear"* (Luke 8:8).

---

> *It is fit neither for the soil nor for the manure pile; it is thrown out. "Whoever has ears to hear, let them hear" (Luke 14:35).*

Nowhere else does it appear in the New Testament until the Book of Revelation, where John uses it seven times in Revelation 2–3, saying, "Whoever has ears, let them hear what the Spirit says to the churches" (Rev. 2:7, 11, 17, 29; 3:6, 13, 22).[18]

> *Whoever has ears, let them hear what the Spirit says to the churches. To the one who is victorious, I will give the right to eat from the tree of life, which is in the paradise of God (Revelation 2:7).*
>
> *Whoever has ears, let them hear what the Spirit says to the churches. The one who is victorious will not be hurt at all by the second death (Revelation 2:11).*
>
> *Whoever has ears, let them hear what the Spirit says to the churches. To the one who is victorious, I will give some of the hidden manna. I will also give that person a white stone with a new name written on it, known only to the one who receives it (Revelation 2:17).*
>
> *Whoever has ears, let them hear what the Spirit says to the churches (Revelation 2:29).*
>
> *Whoever has ears, let them hear what the Spirit says to the churches (Revelation 3:6).*

---

[18] The only other use of this phrase in the Bible is in Revelation 13:9.

*Whoever has ears, let them hear what the Spirit says to the churches* (Revelation 3:13).

*Whoever has ears, let them hear what the Spirit says to the churches* (Revelation 3:22).

The seven *"Whoever has ears, let them hear"* passages in the synoptic gospels have an underlying theme of the coming judgment in AD 70 and the transition from the old covenant to the new covenant. Matthew 13:9, Mark 4:9, and Luke 8:8 all cover the Parable of the Sower, where Jesus mentioned the thirty-, sixty-, and one hundred-fold crop of the seed of the Word of God. The seed of this parable refers to Jesus' Kingdom message about the transition from the old to the new. Many would hear it, but only some would allow that seed to grow in their hearts and produce fruit.

Then, in Matthew 11:15, Jesus states that though John the Baptist was the greatest of the Old Testament prophets, even those who are least in the Kingdom of Heaven are greater than John. This, again, indicates the coming transition between covenants. Likewise, in Mark 13:34, Jesus speaks of the harvest at the end of the age, which refers to the end of the old covenant age and the beginning of the new covenant age.[19] These five passages all directly relate to the covenant transition.

---

[19] For a thorough explanation of why *"the end of the age"* refers to the end of the old covenant, not the end of the world, see my book, *Understanding the Whole Bible*.

The final two verses speak more specifically of what is to come in AD 70. Mark 4:23 talks of things that are concealed being revealed:

*Do you bring in a lamp to put it under a bowl or a bed? Instead, don't you put it on its stand? For whatever is hidden is meant to be disclosed, and whatever is concealed is meant to be brought out into the open. If anyone has ears to hear, let them hear* (Mark 4:21–23).

This is what occurred in AD 70. All the evil actions of the first century Pharisees were about to be brought out into the light, and they were going to be held accountable, even as Jesus declared in Matthew 23:27–28:

*Woe to you, teachers of the law and Pharisees, you hypocrites! You are like whitewashed tombs, which look beautiful on the outside but on the inside are full of the bones of the dead and everything unclean. In the same way, on the outside you appear to people as righteous but on the inside you are full of hypocrisy and wickedness.*

Similarly, in Luke 14:35 He said that when salt loses its saltiness, it is cast out as good for nothing. This also refers to what was about to happen to the Jews in AD 70. All their "good works" would be shown for what they were, because they had rejected their Messiah.

John, recognizing the theme of this statement from Jesus in the synoptic gospels, used it to create a beautiful parallel in his letters to the churches about the coming judgment and covenant transition.

The second repetitive phrase from the synoptic gospels that is mirrored in Revelation is *"Blessed are the...."* Using this pattern, in Matthew 5:3–10, Jesus stated eight blessings that we commonly call the Beatitudes:

> *Blessed are the poor in spirit, for theirs is the kingdom of heaven.*
>
> *Blessed are those who mourn, for they will be comforted.*
>
> *Blessed are the meek, for they will inherit the earth.*
>
> *Blessed are those who hunger and thirst for righteousness, for they will be filled.*
>
> *Blessed are the merciful, for they will be shown mercy.*
>
> *Blessed are the pure in heart, for they will see God.*
>
> *Blessed are the peacemakers, for they will be called children of God.*
>
> *Blessed are those who are persecuted because of righteousness, for theirs is the kingdom of heaven.*

In parallel form, John inserted eight "blessed" statements into the Book of Revelation (see Rev. 1:3; 14:3; 16:15; 19:9; 20:6; 22:7, 14):

> **Blessed** *is the one who reads aloud the words of this prophecy, and* **blessed** *are those who hear it and take to heart what is written in it, because the time is near* (Revelation 1:3).

> *Blessed* are the dead who die in the Lord from now on....They will rest from their labor, for their deeds will follow them (Revelation 14:13).
>
> Look, I come like a thief! *Blessed* is the one who stays awake and remains clothed, so as not to go naked and be shamefully exposed (Revelation 16:15).
>
> *Blessed* are those who are invited to the wedding supper of the Lamb! (Revelation 19:9).
>
> *Blessed* and holy are those who share in the first resurrection. The second death has no power over them, but they will be priests of God and of Christ and will reign with him for a thousand years (Revelation 20:6).
>
> Look, I am coming soon! *Blessed* is the one who keeps the words of the prophecy written in this scroll (Revelation 22:7).
>
> *Blessed* are those who wash their robes, that they may have the right to the tree of life and may go through the gates into the city (Revelation 22:14).

As evident in the use of these parallel phrases from the synoptic gospels, it seems John's *why* in Revelation was, in part, to cover the material he did not cover in his gospel—especially what was relevant to the coming destruction of Jerusalem. Seeing the Book of Revelation as a sort of Olivet Discourse from John, to fill in the gaps left by his gospel, gives us a fuller picture of the purpose of the book as a whole and of the seven letters.

# THE ROAD TO JERUSALEM

The third *why* of John's seven letters to the churches in Revelation is the connection between those cities and the coming destruction of Jerusalem in AD 70. What many modern readers do not realize is that these seven cities were the major cities along the Roman route to Jerusalem.

Ephesus was a major Roman port city, so if Rome were to send an army to Asia Minor (Turkey), Israel, or anywhere in the vicinity, Rome would first send the army to Ephesus. This was the logical port where the Roman army would land. From there, the Roman army would follow the Roman road. The Roman army had built large stone roads, as wide as seventy feet, to facilitate transportation throughout the Empire. These roads were not everywhere, like in our modern world. They followed a specific route according to the usual trade patterns. Each of the seven cities in Revelation 2–3 was along the Roman road. Because of their location, they would be impacted by the army as it came through.

Jewish settlements from the Diaspora existed in each of the cities in Asia Minor. The Jewish people had been scattered throughout the region. As a result, their presence was significant. The Jewish synagogues in these cities had between two thousand and twenty thousand Jewish members. Among them were Christians who had turned to Jesus as the Messiah. So, in these cities, a small Christian church of a few dozen believers would exist within a much larger Jewish population.

The Roman mission was to annihilate the Jews for their revolt against Rome, and the army would be actively killing as many Jews as possible in the cities along their route to Jerusalem. In this, the Romans would not differentiate between

Jews and Jewish Christians. So, the coming of the Roman army presented a real danger to the Christians as well. It was not just the Christians in Israel and Jerusalem who needed to watch for the signs in order to escape the slaughter.

In Matthew 24, Jesus had already warned the Jews of the coming destruction to Jerusalem, and history tells us that the Christians of that region heeded His warnings and escaped the destruction.[20] Now, at Jesus' direction, John gave a similar warning to those in Asia Minor and specifically those along the Roman road. Jesse E. Mills Jr. confirms this:

> Since these cities mentioned in the Apocalypse consisted of Jews from Palestine, and as this would be the route the armies of Rome would take with their object the destruction of the Jews, God favored the pious by sending them a letter of warning to flee the wrath to come.[21]

They needed to be aware of what was coming so they could escape. This is why John began Revelation with these seven letters. As John sat on the Island of Patmos, looking toward Ephesus on the nearby shore, he wrote with great concern for his brothers and sisters in these seven cities. He wrote to prepare them for the immense tragedy coming in their direction. Then, he wrote Revelation 4–22 to expand upon, in the Old Testament style of Ezekiel, Jesus' prophecy in Matthew 24 of the coming destruction of Jerusalem. This is the historical context—the *who, where, when, what,* and *why*—we must understand as we read these seven letters.

---

[20] In their commentaries on Matthew 24, both Adam Barnes and John Gill make note of this.

[21] Mills, 78.

# three

# JESUS REVEALED

Now that we've examined the context of the seven letters and the Book of Revelation as a whole, we must consider John's mysterious naming of this book—*"The revelation of Jesus Christ..."* (Rev. 1:1 ESV). To properly understand John's vision, we must first understand the name he gave it. First and foremost, Revelation was written to reveal or unveil Jesus Christ.

Many books on Revelation begin by saying the vision is about Jesus, but they devote hundreds of pages to discussing the antichrist, the Tribulation, and the end of the world, with little explanation of how these events reveal Jesus. This approach is inconsistent. If Jesus truly is the main focus of the book, these other subjects must be understood in light of Him. The problem, of course, is that many people do not understand how the vision in Revelation actually reveals Jesus. That is because they do not realize that Revelation and the events of AD 70 are about the removal of the old covenant and the full revelation or unveiling of the new covenant Kingdom of Jesus (not the end of the world).

## THE COMING REVELATION

The theme of *revelation* or *unveiling* is crucial to a proper understanding of the book. In fact, it is crucial to an understanding of the entire New Testament. Jesus talked about a future day when He would be revealed, clearly connecting that day with His judgment against Jerusalem:

> *On the day that Lot went out from Sodom it rained fire and brimstone from heaven and destroyed them all. It will be just the same on the day that the Son of Man is revealed* (Luke 17:29–30).

These verses, which are part of Luke's Olivet Discourse, connect the revelation of Jesus with the judgment of the old covenant and Jerusalem. In their letters, the apostles echoed this theme, writing of a soon-approaching day when Jesus would be fully revealed. For example, the apostle Peter wrote:

> *These have come so that the proven genuineness of your faith—of greater worth than gold, which perishes even though refined by fire—may result in praise, glory and honor **when Jesus Christ is revealed**.... Therefore, with minds that are alert and fully sober, set your hope on the grace to be brought to you **when Jesus Christ is revealed** at his coming* (1 Peter 1:7, 13).

This coming that Peter talks about is not the end of the world; it is Jesus' coming in judgment upon the old covenant system and the city of Jerusalem.[22] This coming, Peter promised,

---

[22] For a fuller explanation of why *"coming"* refers to AD 70 and not to Jesus' Second Coming, see my book, *Raptureless.*

would reveal Jesus Christ in fuller measure (see also 1 Pet. 4:13; 5:1). The apostle Paul also spoke of this in multiple places. For example, in his letter to the Thessalonians, he promised:

> *God is just: He will pay back trouble to those who trouble you and give relief to you who are troubled, and to us as well. This will happen* **when the Lord Jesus is revealed** *from heaven in blazing fire with his powerful angels* (2 Thessalonians 1:6–7).

The Thessalonians faced much persecution, and Paul assured them that when Jesus was revealed—in His coming in judgment upon Jerusalem—He would avenge them and give them relief.

To the Corinthians, Paul wrote to encourage them to grow in the spiritual gifts even as they awaited the coming revelation of Jesus: *"Therefore you do not lack any spiritual gift as you eagerly wait for our* **Lord Jesus Christ to be revealed***"* (1 Cor. 1:7). Based on these verses, it seems clear that the early Christians looked forward to a fuller revelation of Jesus that they expected to see with their own eyes. They were not looking ahead to the end of the world but to some other and more immediate revelation of Christ. Paul and Peter had both written, saying, "This is about to happen! He is about to be revealed!" Then, in Revelation, John announced, "This is the unveiling that we have been waiting for; it is just around the corner, and this is how it will happen." That is what John set out as his purpose from the very beginning of Revelation—to describe the soon-coming revelation or unveiling of Jesus they had all been anticipating.

## WHAT WAS HIDING JESUS?

The idea that Jesus needed to be revealed is based on the presupposition that He was hidden or unrevealed. This leads us to ask, *If Jesus needed to be unveiled, what was hiding Him?* The New Testament word translated as "revealed" is the Greek word *apocalypsis*, which means "to unveil, uncover, reveal."[23]

The apostle Paul clearly explains what was veiling Jesus in Second Corinthians 3:

*Now if the ministry that brought death, which was engraved in letters on stone, came with glory, so that the Israelites could not look steadily at the face of Moses because of its glory, transitory though it was, will not the ministry of the Spirit be even more glorious? If the ministry that brought condemnation was glorious, how much more glorious is the ministry that brings righteousness! For what was glorious has no glory now in comparison with the surpassing glory. And if what was transitory came with glory, how much greater is the glory of that which lasts!* (2 Corinthians 3:7–11).

In these verses, Paul set up a comparison between the old covenant and the new covenant. The old, he said, had a measure of glory, but the glory of the new is much greater. Based on this comparison, Paul went on to say:

*Therefore, since we have such a hope, we are very bold. We are not like Moses, who would put a veil over his face to prevent the Israelites from seeing the end of what was*

---

[23] *Strong's Concordance,* Greek #602.

*passing away. But their minds were made dull, **for to this
day the same veil remains when the old covenant is
read.** It has not been removed, because only in Christ is
it taken away. **Even to this day when Moses is read,
a veil covers their hearts.** But whenever anyone turns
to the Lord, **the veil** is taken away. Now the Lord is the
Spirit, and where the Spirit of the Lord is, there is freedom.
And we all, who with **unveiled** faces contemplate the
Lord's glory, are being transformed into his image with
ever-increasing glory, which comes from the Lord, who is
the Spirit* (2 Corinthians 3:12–18).

In other words, the old covenant, the Mosaic covenant, was a
veil that kept Jesus hidden. Even in Paul's day, the old covenant
remained as a veil that kept the Israelites from accurately seeing
Jesus. Here, Paul clearly states that the old covenant had not
yet been removed, and only in Christ would the veil be taken
away. The implication is that for Christ to be revealed, the old
covenant must be removed.

Some might think the old covenant was removed at the
cross, but this passage from Second Corinthians indicates
otherwise. If the old covenant continued to veil Jesus in Paul's
day, that means Jesus' death and resurrection in AD 30 did
not remove the old covenant. Otherwise, Paul would not have
written about the old covenant as though it still existed. On the
cross, when Jesus inaugurated the new covenant, He made the
old covenant obsolete and outdated, but He did not remove
it. This is what Hebrews 8:13 means: *"By calling this covenant
'new,' he has made the first one obsolete; and what is obsolete
and outdated **will soon disappear.**"* It still existed even though
the new covenant had come, but it would not be long until it

was removed altogether. This is the revelation the early Church looked forward to. It is the expectation John addressed when he announced the revelation of Jesus. In effect, he was saying, "I am going to outline the complete collapse and destruction of the old covenant world."

Only through judgment of the old covenant could the new be fully instated. Jesse E. Mills Jr. writes of the need for judgment in the establishment of the new covenant:

"And establish it with judgment." This statement by the prophet Isaiah...states that the authority given the Messiah was to establish it, "it" being the kingdom. Further, Isaiah says that it, the kingdom, will be established with judgment. Therefore, the kingdom was not fully given to the saints until a period when the Messiah would establish it with judgment, and judgment is what we see in Revelation. Therefore, according to Holy Scripture, it was necessary that there be a universal judgment before the kingdom was established and given to the saints.

Quoting from second Psalm, in Acts 13:33–34, Paul declared that God had fulfilled the promise in giving to them "the sure mercies of David." This transaction was somewhat like the removal of presidents in this country. A new man is elected to the office of president, the people vote him into office, but he does not take office the day of his election. It is several months later before you have a new rule....Christ was elected as king on the day of the Cross. He was the new king, but He could not rule until the old king had left office. David and Saul is a classic example of this. Therefore, the new king did not bring his kingdom into full power until the old king left office, then He would establish his kingdom with judgment. This is what verse 7 really means.[24]

This is the key to understanding Revelation—though the old covenant was made obsolete by Christ when He introduced the new covenant in AD 30, the old covenant lingered (along with the Jewish Temple system) until it was destroyed in AD 70. The Jewish Temple and priesthood were the vehicle through which the old covenant was manifested in people's lives. Thus, the destruction of the physical Temple and the Jewish priesthood (including all the genealogical records) permanently ended the old covenant. No longer did the Jews have a Temple where they could practice the sacrificial system. No longer could they identify which Jews were descendants of Aaron and, therefore, rightful priests according to the old covenant. In AD 70, any possibility of continuing on in the Jewish religious system laid out by Moses was completely destroyed. Therefore, after AD 70, though Judaism continued on, it took a completely different form, which is the form it follows to this day.

Through this cataclysmic event in Jewish history, Jesus completely removed the old covenant and fully revealed Himself and His new covenant. As long as the Temple stood in Jerusalem, until AD 70, the old covenant continued to operate in opposition to the new covenant. Thus, from the cross until the destruction of Jerusalem, AD 30–70, the earthly Jerusalem became a "New Egypt," and the Christians experienced a new exodus from the earthly Jerusalem into the new covenant heavenly Jerusalem (see Gal. 4:24–27). John's vision is called the apocalypse (unveiling) of Jesus because it is about the destruction of the old covenant system (see Rev. 4–19) and the finalization of the new covenant

---

[24] Mills, 82–83.

as the only covenant in existence (see Rev. 20–22). It is the unveiling of Jesus Christ and His new covenant by the removal of the veil, which was the old covenant system (see 2 Cor. 3).

With this proper foundation, Revelation 1:1 makes sense. The unveiled new covenant of Jesus is the revelation of Revelation. When we understand the first verse of the book properly, the rest of the book will come into focus.

## THE REVELATION DISPERSED

In the first breath of the Book of Revelation, John states how we should understand its contents. Then he describes an encounter he has with Jesus. This encounter is a key to understanding the seven letters that follow.

*I turned around to see the voice that was speaking to me. And when I turned I saw seven golden lampstands, and among the lampstands was someone like a son of man, dressed in a robe reaching down to his feet and with a golden sash around his chest. The hair on his head was white like wool, as white as snow, and his eyes were like blazing fire. His feet were like bronze glowing in a furnace, and his voice was like the sound of rushing waters. In his right hand he held seven stars, and coming out of his mouth was a sharp, double-edged sword. His face was like the sun shining in all its brilliance. When I saw him, I fell at his feet as though dead. Then he placed his right hand on me and said: "Do not be afraid. I am the first and the Last. I am the living one; I was dead, and now look, I am alive forever and ever! And I hold the keys of death and hades"* (Revelation 1:12–18).

After Jesus appeared to John in this way, He commanded John to write to the seven churches. Each of these letters was dictated to John by Jesus, so they are written in the first person. In them, Jesus uses the visionary revelation of Himself that He had just shown to John to introduce Himself at the beginning of each letter. These self-descriptions are a small selection from the larger description given in Revelation 1:12–18.

1.  Ephesus—He holds the seven stars and walks among the seven lampstands (see Rev. 2:1).

2.  Smyrna—He is the First and Last, the Living One (see Rev. 2:8).

3.  Pergamum—He has the sharp, double-edged sword in His mouth (see Rev. 2:12, 16).

4.  Thyatira—He is the Son of God, whose eyes are like fire and His feet like bronze (see Rev. 2:18).

5.  Sardis—He holds the seven spirits of God and the seven stars (see Rev. 3:1).

6.  Philadelphia—He is holy and true, and He holds the key of David (see Rev. 3:7).

7.  Laodicea—He is the faithful and true witness, the ruler of God's creation (see Rev. 3:14).

Here we see that John (in obedience to Jesus' direction) takes the revelation of Jesus he had just received, and he disperses it in the seven letters. The big picture revelation of the risen Jesus is spread out among the seven churches in Revelation 2–3. This is a beautiful picture of how His body knows in part (see 1 Cor. 13:9). The Spirit takes the big picture revelation of Scripture that

God has given to all of us, and He applies it individually and contextually to us in a way that we will each understand and that will be uniquely meaningful. We all see part of who Jesus is, but none of us sees Him fully or perfectly yet. Thus, we need to work together and learn from each other to begin to see the whole picture of Christ. This is why every joint in the body of Christ must supply its part or its unique perspective (see Eph. 4:16).

In the following seven chapters, which are devoted to the individual letters, we will see the careful logic involved in deciding why each church received the section of the description that it did. For here, it is simply worth noting that Jesus purposefully presented Himself to each of the churches in a way that would be historically and culturally relevant to them. These statements were not just general facts about the nature of Christ; they were specific pieces of revelation intended to deeply connect with the hearts and situations of these churches. This is also how the Spirit speaks to us through prophecy. In these letters, Jesus delivers His prophecies in a very personal manner. He gives each church a piece of revelation regarding what He is like and who He is that is especially applicable to them in their situation. This is a picture of how the gift of prophecy is used within the body of Christ.

Anyone who has prophesied to others can testify that God will use specific words, ideas, and images to get a message to a person in a way that will uniquely and powerfully touch that person's heart. If any other person had received that particular word or image, it probably would not have been nearly as impactful. Often, that word may seem strange to the person delivering it, but the one who receives it knows exactly what it means. This is because God knows exactly what will most speak to each person's heart. He knows each one of us intimately, and He knows how to say, "I love you," to a thousand different people in a thousand different ways. Here, Jesus practically demonstrates for us how personal prophecy is applied and delivered.

In His use of prophecy, we see not only God's heart and loving care for us as individuals but also the beautiful and masterful layering and structure of these letters. After Jesus' great revelation of Himself to John, He made an important statement that helps us understand the structure of the revelation of Christ more completely: *"Write, therefore, what you have seen, what is now and what will take place later"* (Rev. 1:19). This verse divides the content of Revelation into three parts, past, present, and future. The vision of Jesus in Revelation 1:1–18 that John had just seen was *"what you have seen."* That was the past. The letters to the seven churches in Revelation 2–3 was *"what is now."* This was the reality that existed in John's present. The material that John would see in the heavenlies, in Revelation 4–22, was *"what will take place later."* This transition from present to future is made clear by the invitation in Revelation 4:1, *"Come up here, and I will show you what must take place after this."* John only began to see the future after he was pulled up into the heavenlies.

Viewing these timeframes through a historical and contextual grid, we can see that the "what was" and the "what is" of Revelation 1–3 lead up to the "what will be" of the remainder of the book. These are the events of AD 70—the destruction of Jerusalem and the old covenant system.

Here, it is also important to note the symbolic nature of Revelation and this description of Jesus. Take, for example, the statement from Jesus that closes chapter 1:

*The mystery of the seven stars that you saw in my right hand and of the seven golden lampstands is this: The seven stars are the angels of the seven churches, and the seven lampstands are the seven churches* (Revelation 1:20).

Here Jesus tells John that the stars and lampstands are symbolic. They are a mystery that must be interpreted, and He gives the interpretation. The seven lampstands symbolize the seven churches, and the seven stars in His right hand symbolize the angels of those churches. This might seem like a strange arrangement—having an apostle write and deliver letters to spirit beings known as angels—until we realize that stars are used symbolically throughout the Bible to speak of local government,[25] and the Greek word *angelos*, which is translated here as "angels," simply means "messenger or envoy." Knowing this, we can gather that the seven stars/angels refer to the local leadership of the seven churches.

## THE MESSIANIC PROMISE

Not only does each letter begin with a unique description of Jesus, but it ends with a Messianic promise for the "victorious one" or "overcomer." Each of these promises is prefaced by the statement, *"Whoever has ears, let them hear what the Spirit says to the churches."* This, as we discussed in the last chapter, is a phrase borrowed from Jesus' earthly ministry. In the synoptic gospels, He uses it to call attention to the coming covenant transition. Here, He uses it to call attention to the new covenant

---

[25] For example, Joseph's dream in Genesis 37:5–11 was instantly recognized as foretelling his ascendancy to a ruling position, not the literal sun, moon, and stars bowing down to him.

realities that are being made available to His faithful followers. Here are the seven promises He makes:

1. Ephesus—*"To the one who is victorious, I will give the right to eat from the tree of life, which is in the paradise of God"* (Rev. 2:7).

2. Smyrna—*"The one who is victorious will not be hurt at all by the second death"* (Rev. 2:11).

3. Pergamum—*"To the one who is victorious, I will give some of the hidden manna. I will also give that person a white stone with a new name written on it, known only to the one who receives it"* (Rev. 2:17).

4. Thyatira—*"To the one who is victorious and does my will to the end, I will give authority over the nations —that one 'will rule them with an iron scepter and will dash them to pieces like pottery'—just as I have received authority from my Father. I will also give that one the morning star"* (Rev. 2:26–28).

5. Sardis—*"The one who is victorious will, like them, be dressed in white. I will never blot out the name of that person from the book of life, but will acknowledge that name before my Father and his angels"* (Rev. 3:5).

6. Philadelphia—*"The one who is victorious I will make a pillar in the temple of my God. Never again will they leave it. I will write on them the name of my God and the name of the city of my God, the new Jerusalem, which is coming down out of heaven from my God; and I will also write on them my new name"* (Rev. 3:12).

7. Laodicea—*"To the one who is victorious, I will give the right to sit with me on my throne, just as I was victorious and sat down with my Father on his throne"* (Rev. 3:21).

In these promises, the groom (Jesus) speaks to His Bride (the Church), offering Himself to her. Each of these promises is a picture of who Jesus is. So, when He says, *"I will give some of the hidden manna"* (Rev. 2:17) or, *"I will give that one the morning star"* (Rev. 2:28), He is promising Himself. He is promising new covenant union and communion with Him. In this way, He ends each letter with a promise of Himself: "This beautiful part of Me will be available to you when I come in judgment on the old covenant and fully establish the new."

This does not mean that the specific promises were available only to the people in the church that received that letter. It is not, for example, only the victorious ones in Ephesus who get to eat from the tree of life. Instead, all of these promises are applicable to all the believers. They are offered to *"the churches,"* to all believers or the Church as a whole. As the letters were passed from church to church along the Roman road, each church would read all of the letters, and they would see all of what Christ was offering them as their groom. In this way, by spreading the Messianic promises between the letters, Jesus created a recurring theme in which He promises to give Himself to those who faithfully followed Him in the years of persecution and trial leading up to AD 70.

These promises, of course, are also relevant and available to us since we now live fully in the new covenant.[26] Many believers have thought these promises refer to Heaven or the

---

[26] We will discuss this in greater detail in chapter 11.

Millennium. However, when we see that Revelation is about the transition from the old covenant to the new and the full unveiling of Christ, it becomes clear that these promises refer to new covenant realities that were made available in AD 70, at the unveiling of Christ, and are *now* available during our lives on earth. He will not someday give us spiritual authority over the nations. Because of the events of AD 70, He has already given it to us. The same is true of each of these promises. They are current new covenant realities that we can walk in today. They are part of the unveiling of Christ in our lives.

Now that we know what the revelation of Revelation is all about, in the next seven chapters we will examine each of the seven letters according to the local, geographical, and historical contexts of these cities.

# four

# EPHESUS—REVIVAL TOWN

The ancient city of Ephesus now exists only in ruins, but in the first century, Ephesus was the most important city in western Turkey. Once a burgeoning port city, Ephesus now sits seven miles inland, in the shadow of the popular port city of Kusadasi, Turkey. Over the years, the nearby Cayster River filled up the Ephesian harbor with sediment, creating seven miles distance between the town and the shoreline.[27]

In the first century, Ephesus was the great export city at the culmination of the Asiatic caravan route. Trade caravans from the entirety of Turkey came to Ephesus to send their goods throughout the Roman Empire. As such, it was also the perfect landing spot for Roman armies and dignitaries traveling into Asia Minor. The Roman road that ran through Ephesus to the harbor, named the Arcadian Way, was seventy feet wide and lined with magnificent columns. Ephesus was diverse,

---

[27] Fee, *Revelation*, 24.

cosmopolitan, wealthy, and bustling with people. As home to an estimated quarter of a million people, it had the third largest known population of any city in the ancient world.[28] Only Rome and Alexandria surpassed it.

Originally, the city was dedicated to worshipping an Anatolian fertility goddess. Later, it became the home of the cult of the Greek goddess Artemis and the great temple of Artemis, which was one of the seven wonders of the ancient world.[29] Despite its centrality to the pagan religions of the time, Ephesus was also home to a large Jewish population and a growing Christian church. In fact, of all the cities in the New Testament, Ephesus is one of the most central to the story of the early Church (second only to Jerusalem).

Paul visited Ephesus on his second missionary journey in AD 52 (see Acts 18:19–21), and he left Priscilla and Aquila there to continue the work (see Acts 18:19). Apollos also taught in Ephesus (see Acts 18:25). Later, during his third missionary journey, Paul again visited Ephesus and lived there for three years (see Acts 20:31). He saw great fruit for the gospel in Ephesus and the surrounding region. On his way back to Jerusalem, in approximately AD 57, Paul stopped in at Ephesus to say goodbye to the leaders of the church there (see Acts 20:17–38). During his first stretch in prison, in AD 60–63, Paul wrote his letter to the Ephesians. Historians believe that after his release he returned again to Ephesus and, while there, appointed Timothy the leader of the church (see 1 Tim. 1:3). During his second imprisonment, Paul then wrote his two letters to Timothy while Timothy lived in Ephesus.[30]

---

[28] Wright, 11.
[29] Mills, 55.
[30] Hendriksen, 60–61.

Because Ephesus was so central to the growth of the early Church, before looking at its letter in Revelation, we will first examine Paul's interaction with the Ephesians in Acts 19.

## THE GOSPEL AT EPHESUS

In Acts 19:1, we find that Paul traveled to Ephesus through the interior (in other words, not by boat). When he arrived, he encountered a total of twelve followers of Jesus, and he introduced them to the baptism of the Holy Spirit (see Acts 19:2–7). In a city of a quarter of a million people, Paul found only a dozen Christians. It was a very small minority when he arrived. Over the next three months, Paul preached the gospel in the Jewish synagogue, but many of the Jews strongly opposed him (see Acts 19:8–9). Because of this, Paul stopped preaching in the synagogue and instead began having daily discussions in the lecture hall of Tyrannus.

Though Paul began by preaching to the Jews of Ephesus, when they were uninterested, he took his meetings to a public forum. No one knows for sure what the hall of Tyrannus was, but most likely it was a public hall that could be rented for the afternoon. In that climate, the time between 11 a.m. and 4 p.m. was so hot that most people would go back to their houses and rest. This gave the Christians an opportunity to rent this lecture hall during the hours when it normally would have been unused, and they could use it for preaching, teaching, and fellowship.[31]

---

[31] The archeologist Mark Wilson writes, "Public life in Ionian cities like Ephesus ended by noon so Paul would spend the morning working as a tentmaker. At this time Tyrannus might use the auditorium for his own lectures or rent it to others. During the afternoon Paul rented the hall to discuss and debate the Christian gospel with whomever would listen. Since more people would usually be asleep in Ephesus at 1PM than at 1AM, Paul's speaking abilities must have been engaging enough to keep his audience awake at this hour. *Biblical Turkey*, 221.

Paul held these meetings for two years. The fruit of it was that *"all the Jews and Greeks who lived in the province of Asia heard the word of the Lord"* (Acts 19:10). Considering the size of the region, this is an extraordinary statement. The next verses give us a fuller picture of why such a result was possible—Paul was performing great signs and wonders through the Holy Spirit. People were being healed, and evil spirits were being cast out (see Acts 19:11–12). Paul was not just teaching and debating like a secular philosopher; he was demonstrating the supernatural power of God. As a result, people from all over the region flocked to hear the gospel.

Seeing Paul's great success, some non-Christian Jews tried to imitate Paul and use his name to cast out demons. When the seven sons of Sceva, a Jewish priest, tried it, their attempts backfired, and the demonized man beat them senseless (see Acts 19:13–16). This event spread Paul's fame even farther, and the people living in Ephesus *"were all seized with fear, and the name of the Lord Jesus was held in high honor"* (Acts 19:17). People began openly confessing their sins and publicly burning their magic sorcerer's scrolls (see Acts 19:18–19). The significance of this first recorded book burning is summarized in this statement: *"When they calculated the value of the scrolls, the total came to fifty thousand drachmas. In this way the word of the Lord spread widely and grew in power"* (Acts 19:19–20).[32]

---

[32] Although it is not exactly clear what coins are referred to in this passage (Jewish or Greek), many commentators lean toward the Greek currency, estimating the value of these books to be approximately $8,500. Adam Barnes, *Barnes' Notes on the Bible*, Acts 19.

## TROUBLE WITH THE IDOL MAKERS

*"After all this had happened"* (Acts 19:21), as Paul was making plans to leave the region and travel to Jerusalem, trouble surfaced with the Ephesian idol makers. During that time, making idols was a significant source of income for metalworkers. In Ephesus, the main idol being crafted was that of Artemis (or Diana) of the Ephesians, the goddess whose temple was located in Ephesus.[33] Feeling threatened by Paul, an influential silversmith name Demetrius gathered the local craftsmen who made idols for Artemis, and he convinced them that Paul was a threat to their business and to the temple of Artemis:

> *You know, my friends, that we receive a good income from this business. And you see and hear how this fellow Paul has convinced and led astray large numbers of people here in Ephesus and in practically the whole province of Asia. He says that gods made by human hands are no gods at all. There is danger not only that our trade will lose its good name, but also that the temple of the great goddess Artemis will be discredited; and the goddess herself, who is worshiped throughout the province of Asia and the world, will be robbed of her divine majesty* (Acts 19:25–27).

The fact that Paul's preaching could cause such a disturbance among the idol makers shows the extent of his impact. The gospel was truly touching every corner, and those who profited from idol worship felt they might lose their livelihood. Demetrius' speech angered the craftsmen, who began shouting, *"Great is Artemis of the Ephesians!"* (Acts 19:28). The shouting

---

[33] Artemis and Diana were the Greek and Roman names for the same goddess. Today, only one column of the temple of Artemis remains.

spread throughout the city like wildfire. A quarter of a million people were in an uproar, on the brink of a destructive riot. Later, the text tells us that most of the people were caught up in the melee without knowing why they were there or what the problem was (see Acts 19:32). When they got their hands on two of Paul's traveling companions, Gaius and Aristarchus, the people dragged them to the public theater.

When a Jew named Alexander got up to try to calm the crowd, two hours of chanting *"Great is Artemis of the Ephesians!"* ensued. Imagine the hysteria needed to cause thousands of people to shout in unison, in the hot sun, for two hours. Clearly, the crowd was completely out of control (see Acts 19:32–34). In the midst of this, Paul wanted to appear before the crowd in the theater in order to defend himself, but his friends and even the local government leaders begged Paul to stay away (see Acts 19:30–31). Paul's influence had reached to the highest levels of society, and he had made friends with government leaders, who were actively trying to protect him.

To protect Paul, the city clerk scolded the crowd for creating such a disturbance, reminding them of the threat of Roman punishment for rioting. Then he told Demetrius and the craftsmen to take their concerns to court, where they could be addressed by the legal system (see Acts 19:38–41). The clerk also reassured the crowds of Artemis' security as a goddess, saying:

> *Fellow Ephesians, doesn't all the world know that the city of Ephesus is the guardian of the temple of the great Artemis and of her image, which fell from heaven? Therefore, since these facts are undeniable, you ought to calm down and not do anything rash. You have brought*

*these men here, though they have neither robbed temples
nor blasphemed our goddess* (Acts 19:35–37).

Here we find an interesting fact about Artemis of the
Ephesians. In mainland Greece, the goddess Artemis was
worshipped as the daughter of Zeus and the twin sister of
Apollo. She was known as a hunter, assistant to midwives, and
protector of young children. But Asia Minor had its own version
of Artemis, and it differed greatly from the Greek Artemis.
Some scholars believe this image from heaven was actually
a meteorite that the locals deified. Others believe this phrase
was used commonly to refer to any deity to make it seem more
legitimate.[34] The Ephesian Artemis was worshipped almost
exclusively as a fertility goddess, and her idols are very different
from the idols of Artemis in Greece. Instead of the nimble
huntress, the Ephesian Artemis is portrayed as a many-breasted
mummy-shaped woman.

With this background in place, let's consider the Revelation
letter to the Ephesians.

## SEVEN STARS AND LAMPSTANDS

The letter starts out with a description of Jesus: *"To the angel
of the church in Ephesus write: These are the words of him who
holds the seven stars in his right hand and walks among the
seven golden lampstands."* To the Ephesians, Jesus emphasizes
His role as the one who holds the sevens stars and lampstands.
These seven stars and lampstands, according to Revelation 1,

---

[34] C.C. Wylie and J.R. Naiden, "The image which fell down from Jupitar,"
*Popular Astronomy*, 44 (1936), 514; http://articles.adsabs.harvard.edu/full/seri/
PA.../0044//0000514.000.html (accessed Sept. 24, 2015).

are symbols. The seven lampstands are the seven churches. This echoes Jesus' description of believers as lights in the world:

> *You are the light of the world. A town built on a hill cannot be hidden. Neither do people light a lamp and put it under a bowl. Instead they put it on its stand, and it gives light to everyone in the house* (Matthew 5:14–15).

The lampstands are the churches, and the seven stars are the angels at each church, or their local leaders.[35] So, it seems that Jesus was reminding them that He holds the local church leaders in His hand. The right hand is the one that reaches the heart. It's the one that symbolizes power, strength, justice, and righteousness. Thus, this statement was meant as an encouragement and comfort.

The fact that He holds the leaders while walking among the churches also shows the unity of these churches as the larger body of Christ. It reminds us of Jesus' promise in Matthew 18:20: *"For where two or three gather in my name, there am I with them."* Though they are in separate cities, He is with and among them, unifying them in His bigger purposes. As they faced impending difficulty, this would remind them that they are not alone. Not only is Jesus with them, but they also have the community of believers throughout the region. This promise extends beyond the Ephesians to all seven churches. Jesus holds *all* the leaders and walks among *all* the churches. He knows them intimately and cares about them deeply, so He introduces the first letter, and the whole series of letters, by emphasizing His loving presence and care.

---

[35] As mentioned in chapter 3, stars are a common biblical symbol for government, and the Greek word translated as "angels" simply means "messengers."

## FALSE APOSTLES

Jesus then commends the Ephesian church for their success in several areas:

> *I know your deeds, your hard work and your perseverance. I know that you cannot tolerate wicked people, that you have tested those who claim to be apostles but are not, and have found them false. You have persevered and have endured hardships for my name, and have not grown weary* (Revelation 2:2–3).

First, He praises their perseverance in the face of hardship and persecution. Second, He praises their refusal to tolerate wicked people and false apostles. We know the Ephesian church had seen its share of spiritual conflict, including the protests of the idol maker Demetrius (see Acts 19) and the scandal of the woman of the Artemis cult who was disrupting Timothy's church meetings (see 1 Tim. 2:11–12). Yet neither of these individuals would have been considered false apostles. The danger Jesus referred to was from within the church. When Paul left, he had warned the elders at Ephesus:

> *I know that after I leave, savage wolves will come in among you and will not spare the flock. Even from your own number men will arise and distort the truth in order to draw away disciples after them* (Acts 20:29–30).

It seems this is exactly what had happened, and the Ephesians had handled the situation righteously, not allowing these false apostles to remain among them.[36] From the historical

---

[36] Terry, 292.

record, the person who most likely fits this description was a false teacher named Cerinthus. About him, the early Church historian, Eusebius, wrote:

> But Cerinthus, by means of revelations which he pretended to such wonderful things, and pretended they were written by a great apostle, and claimed the revelation was shown him by an angel, and, asserting that after the resurrection of Christ there would be an earthly kingdom of Christ, Cerinthus being an enemy to the Divine word, with a view to deceive men, he said there would be a space of a thousand years for celebrating nuptial festivals. It is highly probable that Cerinthus, the same that established the heresy that bears his name, designedly affixed the name of John to his forgery.[37]

According to Eusebius, Cerinthus impersonated the apostle John and spread the false teaching now known as pre-millennialism—the idea that Jesus would return and reign over an earthly kingdom for a literal one thousand years. Cerinthus is the earliest person known to history who taught this, and he falsely attached the apostle John's name to his teaching in order to gain more influence.

The third-century theologian, Hippolytus, tells us that "Cerinthus was the ringleader of Paul's Judaizing antagonist in Jerusalem."[38] Paul faced a great deal of trouble from Judaizers who tried to combine the old covenant and the new covenant during the first century. These Judaizers, led by Cerinthus, would bring confusion into churches after Paul had left. Thus,

---

[37] Eusebius, ch. 28, 113–114.
[38] Mills, 60.

it is possible, when Paul warned the Ephesian leaders about the *"grievous wolves,"* that he actually had Cerinthus in mind.

Irenaeus, the Church father, recorded an anecdote that shows the severity of John's opinion of Cerinthus. John was released from his exile on Patmos in AD 68, after Nero committed suicide and the next emperor, Galba, declared a pardon for those in Asia Minor. So, John returned to Ephesus and took leadership of the church there. One day, John entered a public bath to wash, but when he realized that Cerinthus was there, he quickly jumped from the water, saying, *"Let us flee, lest the bath fall in, as long as Cerinthus, that enemy of truth, is within."*[39] Clearly, John felt strongly about this man who had attached his name to false teachings. It would seem that even the apostle of love abhorred Cerinthus.

What is important here is that, in the time between Paul's warning and Jesus' letter to the Ephesians, they had been diligent to test those who called themselves apostles and to cast out the false ones. This is a tremendous commendation, because as we know from Paul's letters, many of the early churches were confused and deceived by the Judiazers.

## FORSAKEN FIRST LOVE

After this praise, Jesus rebukes the Ephesian church for having lost their first love:

> *Yet I hold this against you: You have forsaken the love you had at first. Consider how far you have fallen! Repent and do the things you did at first. If you do not repent, I will*

---

[39] Ibid.

> *come to you and remove your lampstand from its place* (Revelation 2:4–5).

This is a big enough deal that Jesus actually threatens to remove their lampstand, or their church presence. As Paul pointed out to the Corinthians, *"If I speak in the tongues of men or of angels, but do not have love, I am only a resounding gong or a clanging cymbal"* (1 Cor. 13:1). Without love, their witness was compromised, and they were in danger of losing their lampstand, or their local presence as a church. This doesn't mean Jesus was threatening to destroy them. Instead, by removing their lampstand He would simply be permitting the full manifestation of what they had already chosen in their hearts. After all, if they were not walking in love, they could not possibly be His representatives.

MODERN APPLICATION: Without love, our witness as Christians is compromised. If we are not walking in love, we cannot possibly represent Christ accurately. (See 1 Corinthians 13.)

Jesus' purpose here is not to shame the Ephesians but to call them back to Him. He is pleading with them to rekindle the fire of their first love so that they can continue on in the work of the Kingdom in Ephesus. When Paul first visited Ephesus, the church there experienced great power. They were seeing signs and wonders and being a tremendous witness for the gospel in the entire region. The disciples were being built up and fit together into a household of God (see Eph. 2).

One commentator, David Chilton, suggests that the phrase, *"see how far you have fallen,"* was a subtle reference to the silting problem at Ephesus. The Cayster River had brought so much dirt into the harbor that it was causing the city to move back away from the harbor. In those days, they had developed a dredging system so that the harbor remained at Ephesus. But in the years since then, when people stopped dredging the harbor, it filled with dirt, and eventually Ephesus was seven miles inland. This is a compelling picture of what Jesus was communicating to the church at Ephesus. He was telling them to dredge the harbor of their hearts in order to remove the dirt that was pushing them away from the Kingdom. "Do you see how far you have fallen away from the harbor? Go back to your first love," He says. Paul had invested a great deal into the church in this city, and Jesus is calling them to return to what they had received from him.

## NICOLAITAN PRACTICES

After this correction, Jesus adds another praise for the Ephesians: *"But you have this in your favor: You hate the practices of the Nicolaitans, which I also hate"* (Rev. 2:6). The mystery of the Nicolaitans is a fascinating one. We have very little historical information to tell us who they were and what God hated about them. According to Irenaeus, the Nicolaitans were founded by Nicholas, the proselyte of Antioch, who was one of the seven deacons chosen to serve at the tables in Acts 6:5.[40] This Nicholas started as a pagan, then converted to Judiasm, and then converted to Christianity. He was chosen to serve as a deacon, but then, according to Irenaeus, he apostatized. He walked away from Christianity and started a movement called the Nicolaitans.

We do not know for sure what the Nicolaitans taught, but their name means "conqueror of the laity" or "conqueror of the

---

[40] Irenaeus. *Against Heresies*, book 1, 26:3; book 3, 10:7. Also, Mills, 62; Robertson, 300.

people." Thus, it would seem that their heresy related to church government. David Chilton and Watchman Nee both agree that the Nicolaitan heresy had something to do with hierarchical control of other people.[41] Nee said, "Nicolaitans, then, refers to a group of people who esteem themselves higher than the common believers."[42] The man who had converted from paganism to Judaism to Christianity and been given a position to serve eventually became a dominator of people. He fell from being a servant-hearted man and started a movement based on power and control over others. It is a tragic story.

Though the Nicolaitan heresy flourished in some churches (as we will see later in Pergamum), in Ephesus it was soundly squelched. Perhaps this is because the apostle Paul had spent so much time teaching the Ephesians what the Kingdom of God is like. In his letter to the Ephesians, we read his command to mutually submit to one another (see Eph. 5:21). And when he laid out the five-fold leadership of the Church, he taught that the role of apostles, prophets, evangelists, pastors, and teachers is for serving and equipping other believers (see Eph. 4:11–13), not for controlling them. In Ephesus, Paul laid a foundation for servant-hearted leadership, not hierarchy and domineering leadership. Because of this, the Ephesians hated the Nicolaitan control and abuse just as much as God did.

> MODERN APPLICATION:
> God desires servant-hearted leaders who will empower and equip the believers, not control them.

---

[41] In Greek, *iVik-ohzos* means "conqueror of the people," Chilton, 98.
[42] Nee, 17.

# THE TREE OF LIFE

Jesus then ends His letter to the Ephesians with this Messianic promise:

> *Whoever has ears, let them hear what the Spirit says to the churches. To the one who is victorious, I will give the right to eat from the tree of life, which is in the paradise of God* (Revelation 2:7).

The tree of life and paradise of God are featured in the Genesis creation account. In the middle of the Garden of Eden, the earthly paradise, was the tree of life, which Adam and Eve were free to eat from (see Gen. 2:9). This tree granted eternal life, so when Adam and Eve sinned, they lost access to the garden and the tree. However, when Jesus came and restored humanity's relationship with God, He also restored access to the tree of life (and eternal life) for all who believe in Him. We see this at the end of Revelation, where the tree of life is in the midst of the paradise of God and available to those who wash their robes, who receive salvation from Christ (see Rev. 22:2, 14). This is the meaning of Jesus' promise to the believers of the right to eat from the tree of life. It symbolizes restored relationship with God and eternal life.

This promise, however, also had a local application that made it especially meaningful to the Ephesians. The temple of Artemis in Ephesus was built with 127 immense pillars designed to look like an eternal (stone) forest. In the center of the temple, an opening in the roof allowed light to shine down on a garden. This sacred garden, called the *Parádeisos* (Greek for "paradise"), was supposedly where Artemis had fallen to earth. Inside the *Parádeisos* was a sacred tree that the locals believed

Artemis originated from (the Artemis idol was made of wood). This tree was also a place of sanctuary for criminals. Those who came within a certain distance of the tree were free from capture and punishment. Some of the local coins had an image of this tree engraved on them, so the idea of this tree of sanctuary was regularly in the Ephesian conscience.[43] The similarities to God's tree of life and God's paradise garden are obvious, but what Jesus offers is better.

When we know the cultural context, we can see that Jesus was declaring to the Ephesian Christians, "I am better than Artemis. I have the true paradise, and I offer the tree of life. My followers receive the fruit from My tree. In the center of My Church resides the true paradise." Jesus points to the local idolatry and false worship that surrounded the believers of Ephesus, and He declares Himself greater. This is something Jesus did not only in Ephesus but in each of the letters. He identifies Himself according to the local context and then shows how He trumps the local religion. Though to the believers of that day it may have seemed impossible, history has shown that the Kingdom of God has prevailed while the worship of Artemis has vanished. Even the Artemis temple, once one of the Seven Wonders of the World, is now in ruins. Only one conglomerate pillar remains.

Here, Jesus reminds His followers who face persecution (then and now) that they have received His eternal Kingdom. Unlike human temples, Christ's Kingdom, the paradise of God, will never crumble and fall. It is truly eternal, and all who follow Jesus will find forever life within.

---

[43] Wright, 12.

# SMYRNA–PERSECUTED CHURCH

# five

Heading fifty miles north from Ephesus, the next population center was the port city of Smyrna, along the Aegean Sea.[44] Smyrna was the second largest city in Asia Minor (after Ephesus), and it was reputedly the most beautiful. Today, it is the modern city of Izmir, home to approximately four million people. Of all the seven cities, Smyrna has the most significant modern presence, in part because it never revolted against Rome. Though Ephesus had several skirmishes with the Roman authorities, Smyrna was always loyal to Rome.[45] The Roman writer Cicero called Smyrna "the city of our most faithful and most ancient allies."[46] Smyrna is also known as the home of the poet Homer, author of *The Iliad* and *The Odyssey*.[47]

---

[44] Smyrna was "...a city about fifty miles north of Ephesus at the head of a deep gulf, and therefore with an excellent harbor." Fee, *Revelation*, 29.

[45] "From the very beginning of Rome's rise to power, even before its days of greatness, Smyrna was its loyal ally and was recognized as such by Rome." Hendriksen, 63.

[46] Wilson, *Biblical Turkey*, 312.

[47] Ibid., 311.

The name *Smyrna* comes from the word *myrrh*,[48] which was a common perfume in the ancient world. It was also used to embalm and perfume dead bodies (including Jesus' body, see John 19:39). The meaning of Smyrna is a coincidental undertone to the fact that the church there faced tremendous persecution. As a result, Jesus' letter to them revolves around themes of death and resurrection.

## THE RESURRECTED ONE

In fact, Jesus introduces Himself along these lines, saying: *"To the angel of the church in Smyrna write: These are the words of him who is the First and the Last, who died and came to life again"* (Rev. 2:8). Because the believers in Smyrna were suffering persecution from local Jewish leaders, their biggest concern was the question of resurrection. If they were martyred, would they experience eternal life? In this life-and-death context, Jesus identifies Himself as the one who has already experienced death and has been resurrected into eternal life. His example is also a promise, as Paul said to the Corinthians:

> *If only for this life we have hope in Christ, we are of all people most to be pitied. But Christ has indeed been raised from the dead, the firstfruits of those who have fallen asleep. For since death came through a man, the resurrection of the dead comes also through a man. For as in Adam all die, so in Christ all will be made alive* (1 Corinthians 15:19–22).

If Jesus was resurrected, His followers would also be resurrected. This was a powerful and comforting promise to the

---

[48] Nee, 21.

believers of Smyrna. Jesus could identify with their plight. He too had suffered persecution and been martyred, and He had overcome death on their behalf. Because of His presence with them, though they might physically die, they would live forever with God.

Also, Jesus' description of Himself as the one who was dead and came back to life may be an allusion to the history of the city of Smyrna, which had been previously destroyed and rebuilt.[49] In 600 BC, Smyrna was destroyed by the Lydian king Alyattes, and it lay in ruins until the 300s BC, when it was rebuilt by Alexander the Great.[50] This decision to rebuild was the result of a dream Alexander the Great had while visiting Smyrna. In the dream, two nymphs, known as Revenge and Retribution, who were representatives of the goddess Nemesis, visited Alexander. We do not know the contents of his dream, but there is an ancient fountain that commemorates where he slept when he had the dream to rebuild Smyrna.[51] As a city, then, Smyrna had experienced a metaphorical resurrection. Thus, this theme of death and resurrection was one the believers of Smyrna could uniquely relate to on multiple levels. In light of their history, Jesus declares to the believers of Smyrna that He is greater than Alexander the Great. He, Jesus, is the true Great King who possesses resurrection power.

## PERSECUTION AND THE SYNAGOGUE OF SATAN

After comforting the believers with His identity as the resurrected one, Jesus got right to the issue at hand, persecution:

---

[49]  Wright, 18.
[50]  Wilson, *Biblical Turkey*, 311.
[51]  Ibid., 311–312.

*"I know your afflictions and your poverty—yet you are rich! I know about the slander of those who say they are Jews and are not, but are a synagogue of Satan"* (Rev. 2:9). Here, Jesus refers to two forms of persecution—affliction and poverty.[52] Though the Christians were poor and persecuted, Jesus encourages them that, in His Kingdom, they are rich.

The Christians at Smyrna suffered at the hands of the local Jewish leaders, those John referred to as the *"synagogue of Satan."* Prior to AD 70, "the main adversaries of Christianity were the Jews." Of all the cities in Asia Minor, Smyrna had the largest Jewish population (thousands strong), and therefore, the Christians there faced more difficulty than most.[53] The Jews of Smyrna held a great deal of power, and they actively persecuted the Christians, many of whom had probably come out of the Jewish community. In response to this persecution, Jesus says of these people, "They say they are Jews, but they are not." This statement echoes the words of Paul in Romans:

> *A person is not a Jew who is one only outwardly, nor is circumcision merely outward and physical. No, a person is a Jew who is one inwardly; and circumcision is circumcision of the heart, by the Spirit, not by the written code...* (Romans 2:28–29).

In other words, the true Jew is the one who has received Jesus and His new creation heart. Whether or not a person is Jewish by descent no longer matters; what matters is belief in the Messiah and His new covenant. That's what makes a person a "true Jew."

---

[52] Persecution was accompanied by poverty because "people were often thrown out of employment as a result of the very fact of their conversion." Hendriksen, 64.

[53] Gregg, 67.

This is why Jesus said that the Jews who persecuted the Christians were not Jews at all. Though they had Jewish genes, they had deliberately chosen against their Messiah and stepped outside the household of faith. Therefore, they were "false Jews."

> MODERN APPLICATION:
> Family heritage does not matter in the new covenant. The "true Jew" is the person who embraces Christ and His new covenant, regardless of ethnic background. This means that Israel as a nation no longer has a special place with God. In the new covenant, both Jew and gentile become one in Christ by faith. (See Galatians 3:28.)

Jesus' words here also echo back to His dispute with the religious leaders in John 8, where He insisted that, instead of Abraham or God, their true father was the devil (see John 8:31–47). The true children of Abraham are not just physical descendants but those who are descendants by faith. Paul makes this clear again in Romans 9:6–8:

> For not all who are descended from Israel are Israel. Nor because they are his descendants are they all Abraham's children. On the contrary, "It is through Isaac that your offspring will be reckoned." In other words, it is not the children by physical descent who are God's children, but it is the children of the promise who are regarded as Abraham's offspring.

This was a huge shift in the first century. For thousands of years, the Jews as an ethnic group had thought of themselves as God's chosen people based on their Jewish heritage and covenant with God. Now, God was changing that. He was calling His people of faith, those who had embraced Jesus (whether Jew or gentile), out from among the ethnic Jews. These Christian

Jews were the true Jews, while the old covenant Jews were false Jews who had turned their backs on God.

God had sent His Son, the Messiah, to the Jews, but most of them had rejected Him. In so doing, they abandoned their place within God's people. Those who were left, the "true Jews," were the Jews of the heart, whether they were physically descendants of Abraham or not. Theologian N.T. Wright summarizes this well:

> In western Turkey...there was a large and lively synagogue community as well, whose members did not believe that Jesus was God's Messiah, sent to Israel to announce God's kingdom, and raised from the dead to prove the point. This was especially so when members of the synagogue, not content with their own rejection of Jesus, actively blasphemed him, perhaps calling down curses upon him. Who, therefore, is the true Jew? Paul already gave the answer in Romans 2:25–29: the one who is the "Jew" in the heart.[54]

This question—*who is a true Jew?*—has been hotly debated since the beginning of Christianity, and it is still debated today. Many modern Christians want to give ethnic Jews a special place in God's Kingdom, but as William Hendriksen points out:

> How anyone can say that the Jews of today are still, in a very special and glorious and preeminent sense, God's people, is more than we can understand. God Himself calls those who reject the Savior and persecute true believers "the synagogue of Satan."[55]

---

[54] Wright, 17.
[55] Hendriksen, 65.

Jesus called the Jewish people of the first century who continued to reject His Kingship *"a synagogue of Satan."* The new covenant Kingdom is not about natural lineage but about faith. We do not enter His Kingdom through natural birth but through the spiritual birth Jesus described to Nicodemus (see John 3:1–21). Thus, in His letter to the persecuted church in Smyrna, Jesus reassures the believers that they are the true Jews, His true family of faith.

## TESTED FOR TEN DAYS

Jesus continues by warning the believers of a coming trial: *"Do not be afraid of what you are about to suffer. I tell you, the devil will put some of you in prison to test you, and you will suffer persecution for ten days..."* (Rev. 2:10). Gordon Fee suggests the mysterious *ten days* is a Hebrew idiom and "...is to be understood as indicating that it would be for a limited time only."[56] Milton Terry agrees, pointing to the biblical precedent: "The *ten days* are to be taken as a symbolical number, here indicative of a limited period of time (comp. Matt xxiv, 22; Dan. i, 12, 14; Gen. xxiv, 55)."[57]

Watchman Nee also points to the biblical precedent as proof that ten days is a symbol for a short time:

In the Bible ten days are spoken of many times. In Genesis 24:55 there are "ten days." When the servant wanted to take Rebecca with him, Rebecca's brother and mother requested that she stay with them for at least ten days. When Daniel and his friends would not allow

---

[56] Fee, *Revelation*, 32.
[57] Terry, 297.

themselves to be defiled by the king's food, they asked the officer in charge to try them for ten days (Dan. 1:11–12). So "ten days" in the Bible has a meaning, that is, a very short time.[58]

What Nee seems to overlook is that, in both cases he mentions, the ten days referred to a short period of *testing*. In His letter to Smyrna, Jesus also uses the ten days idiom to represent a short period of testing that was about to come upon them. By using this idiom, Jesus was reminding the believers of individuals in Scripture who had also faced a "ten day" test. Each of these had been successful, and Jesus reminds the believers in Smyrna of that heritage and encourages them that they, too, will be successful.

History does not tell us what this short time of testing referred to, but it is reasonable to think Jesus may have been referring to the coming Roman armies. As a city with a large Jewish population, Smyrna would suffer greatly as the Romans passed through on their mission to obliterate the Jews. It is quite likely that Christians were caught up in the Roman rampage as well, since many of the early Christians were Jewish by race. After the Roman destruction of the Jews, the once large and thriving synagogue of Smyrna was most likely on the brink of extinction. Certainly, the Jews who remained would not have had the same strength or ability to persecute the Christians.

## RESURRECTION AWAITS THE FAITHFUL

Jesus follows His warning about the coming test with a Messianic promise:

---

[58] Nee, 29–30.

> *...Be faithful, even to the point of death, and I will give you life as your victor's crown. Whoever has ears, let them hear what the Spirit says to the churches. The one who is victorious will not be hurt at all by the second death* (Revelation 2:10–11).

Here, Jesus promises that those who are martyred—who are faithful unto death, even as Jesus was (see Phil. 2:7–8)—will receive the crown of life. N.T. Wright suggests that this phrase may mean "life as a crown." The city of Smyrna was spoken of as a city with a crown because of the way its buildings appeared on the hill it was built on.[59] In a similar way, believers will reign with Christ, crowned with His life. As Romans 5:17 says, "*...how much more will those who receive God's abundant provision of grace and of the gift of righteousness reign in life through the one man, Jesus Christ!*"

Jesus adds, using a statement that many have found cryptic, that those who die will not be hurt by the second death. The first death was the spiritual death humanity experienced through Adam's sin. The second death is the lake of fire (see Rev. 20:14). Instead of experiencing the lake of fire, believers will be resurrected, found in the book of life, and crowned with life at the Lord's coming (see 2 Tim. 4:8; 1 Pet. 5:4). David Chilton provides even greater clarity to this passage:

Revelation 20:6 states that those who are not hurt by the "Second Death" are the same as those who partake of "the First Resurrection"; and that they are priests and kings with Christ—a blessing St. John has already affirmed to be a present reality (1:6).[60]

---

[59] Wright, 18.
[60] Chilton, 104.

This means, the first resurrection does not refer to the resurrection at the end of the world but to the spiritual resurrection we experience when Christ makes us spiritually alive in Him (see Eph. 2:1, 4–6). In this first resurrection, the believer escapes judgment (the second death) and *"has crossed over from death to life"* (John 5:24).[61] Jesus opens His letter to Smyrna by identifying Himself as the one who has been resurrected, and He ends the letter by passing the promise of resurrection on to His followers. Though they face terrible persecution, and some of them will die for their faith, they can hold on to His promise of resurrection life.

---

[61] Ibid.

# six

# PERGAMUM–ROMAN CAPITAL

The third city, Pergamum, the seat of the Roman governor of the whole region,[62] was seventy miles north of Smyrna and fifteen miles inland. Today it is the city of Bergama, Turkey. Although Ephesus was the major export and trade center, all the authority of the region was connected to Pergamum. As one commentator puts it, "If Ephesus was the 'New York City' of Asia, Pergamum was its 'Washington, D.C.'"[63] Pergamum was home to a university for medical study and a famous library, and the Roman philosopher, Pliny, called it "the most illustrious city of Asia."[64]

Pergamum's library contained 200,000 volumes, making it the second largest library in the world at that time; only the library in Alexandria surpassed it. But the volumes did

---

[62] Wright, 20.

[63] Gregg, 68.

[64] Wilson, *Biblical Turkey*, 281; Robertson, 303.

not remain in the Pergamum library. In 48 BC, Julius Caesar devastated the library in Alexandria in his attack of Egypt. When Mark Antony came to power, he generously restored the great library of Alexandria by giving Queen Cleopatra all the volumes from Pergamum (in 41 BC) as a wedding gift![65]

Before Julius Caesar destroyed the Alexandrian library, the two libraries were competing to be the biggest. Because of this, the Alexandrians put a trade embargo on all Papyrus in order to hinder the Pergamum library's growth. Undaunted, the people of Pergamum created a new material for writing. Originally known as *charta pergamene*, today it is called *parchment*.[66]

In 29 BC, Pergamum erected the very first temple for worshiping a Roman Emperor in honor of Caesar Augustus.[67] Not only was Pergamum the seat of the Roman government of the region, but it was also the seat of the Imperial cult. Here, all citizens were required to offer incense to the image of the emperors and say, "Caesar is Lord."[68]

Alongside their emperor worship, the people of Pergamum also worshipped the god Asclepius, a healing god in the form of a serpent. The connection between healing and snakes was not unique to the Greeks. In fact, in the Old Testament, Moses even used a bronze serpent on a staff as an agent of God's healing for Israel (see Num. 21:4–9). Hundreds of years later, the Israelites took that same bronze serpent, which was simply a tool of God, and they began to worship it as an idol (see 2 Kings 18:4). So, something that started as a blessing later became a curse. In

---

[65] Wilson, *Biblical Turkey*, 286.

[66] Ibid., 283.

[67] Fee, *Revelation*, 33.

[68] Hendricksen, 66.

the first century, Christians viewed the serpent as a symbol of Satan. Further, Asclepius' title was *Soter*, or Savior, which put his worshippers immediately at odds with the early Christians who were performing healing miracles in the name of their Savior, Jesus Christ.[69]

Connected to the worship of Asclepius was a health resort, the Asclepieion, where people came for water baths, music, prayer, and dream interpretation. It even had a 3,500-seat theater for music therapy and a sleep chamber where people could come to sleep and receive prophetic dreams (which were most likely drug induced).[70] A man named Galen, who is considered the Father of Pharmacy, hailed from Pergamum and was associated with the Asclepius healing center.

The city was built in such a way that its acropolis sat on a high hill in the middle of the city, making its many temples and altars prominent and visible on the skyline for miles in all directions.[71] Alongside the temple dedicated to the Emperors, the massive altar of the god Zeus featured prominently in the religious landscape. The large altar (which is now in a museum in Berlin) would have had a continual cloud of smoke rising from it, due to the ongoing animal sacrifices offered on it. This must have been a spectacular and intimidating view from the city in the valley.

The temple to the goddess Athena, the goddess of victory, also sat near the top of the hill. Also, a massive temple to the Egyptian god Serapis (as well as some other Egyptian deities, including the goddess Isis) stood on the acropolis in Pergamum.

---

[69] Wilson, *Biblical Turkey*, 290.
[70] Mills, 57.
[71] Wright, 20.

Today, this temple is known as the Red Basilica. It contained a massive cult statue, at least thirty-three feet tall, that the temple priests could make "talk" by entering the base of the statue and speaking through a pipe. Thus, the statue seemed to speak to the people.[72]

N.T. Wright describes the impact of this environment on the church at Pergamum:

> Many local inhabitants in the first century must have been proud of all this. But for the little Christian community it represented a threat—and a threat with which, it seemed, the Christians were not coping particularly well.[73]

The towering acropolis with its temples and altars, with its pillars of smoke and talking idols, must have seemed overwhelming and intimidating to the believers trying to stand up for Christ. Considering the proliferation of temples and altars to false gods, the emperor worship, and the presence of the Roman government itself, it is no surprise Jesus describes Pergamum as the place *"where Satan dwells."*[74]

## SHARP DOUBLE-EDGED SWORD

In this environment, Jesus introduces Himself in militant fashion: *"To the angel of the church in Pergamum write: These are the words of him who has the sharp, double-edged sword"* (Rev. 2:12). Jesus chooses to use this portion of His description

---

[72] Wilson, *Biblical Turkey*, 290. It is likely that similar statues of Nero, which were set up in the public markets, were also made to "talk." Thus, the image of the Beast was able to utter words in Revelation 13.

[73] Ibid.

[74] Hendricksen, 66.

from Revelation 1 here because it would have been especially relevant to the Christians in Pergamum. Living in the Roman capital of Asia Minor, the people of Pergamum would have known and feared the power of the sword. They would have understood that Jesus was declaring Himself to be the true authority in Pergamum. He is the one with the real power, holding the greatest sword. He is the king over all other kings.

## THE THRONE OF SATAN AND THE DEATH OF ANTIPAS

After stating His authority, Jesus then reassures the believers that He knows the difficulty of their situation, and He praises them for remaining faithful:

> *I know where you live—where Satan has his throne. Yet you remain true to my name. You did not renounce your faith in me, not even in the days of Antipas, my faithful witness, who was put to death in your city—where Satan lives* (Revelation 2:13).

Here, He specifically addresses the two main concerns in the minds of the Pergamum believers: living in the shadow of Satan's throne and the recent death of Antipas.

As mentioned earlier, Pergamum could have been considered the throne of Satan for several reasons. Commentators agree that the most likely of the reasons for this label from Jesus was the existence of the Roman government and the Imperial Cult of Emperor worship. About this, David Chilton says:

It was here that Satan has established his official seat or chair of state. As Rome had become the center for

Satan's activity in the west, so Pergamum had become his "throne" in the East.[75]

Because Pergamum was both the Roman capital in Asia Minor and the origin of emperor worship in Asia Minor, Satan did not just reside there, but his throne, the "seat of power of the king or judge" was there.[76] This was the place of government for the region, and through the Roman Emperors, Satan influenced all of Asia Minor.

A second and less prominent reason for this title was the local shrine to the healing god, Asclepius, whose symbol was a serpent and whose title was *Soter*, or Savior. In his temple, non-venomous snakes were allowed to roam freely. The god Asclepius was also typically depicted with a serpent entwined around a staff, which has carried over to the modern symbol for medicine. While the Asclepius cult viewed their snake god positively, the Bible tells us the identity of the spirit behind Asclepius—*"that ancient serpent, who is the devil, or Satan"* (Rev. 20:2).[77]

People would travel great distances to visit the temple and bathhouse of Asclepius in hopes of being healed and receiving dreams. Because of this, there was a very real spiritual battle between the demonic spirit of Asclepius and the followers of Jesus. The question was, who is the real savior and healer— Asclepius or Jesus? When Jesus came as the Savior (*Soter*) of the World, that term was already being used by Asclepius. So, Jesus' assumption of that title was a direct challenge: "No, not you, Asclepius. I am the Savior of the world." Because of the

---

[75] Chilton, 106.
[76] Robertson, 304.
[77] Wright, 20.

popularity of the Asclepius cult, healing people in Jesus' name could get the believers in serious trouble. It was seen as a direct challenge to their god.

This is where Antipas came in. Most commentaries do not say much about Antipas, but from the apocryphal book, *The Acts of Antipas*, we learn that Antipas was the bishop of Pergamum. The apostle John had appointed Antipas prior to his exile on Patmos, and while John was gone, Antipas was martyred.[78]

Antipas had practiced medicine as a local dentist, and when people came to Antipas with dental problems, sometimes he would cure them by natural means, but sometimes he would pray for them in the name of Jesus. Demons would come out of people, and they would be healed. Regardless of how people were healed, Antipas did not charge his patients a fixed rate; he only accepted freewill offerings.

Antipas' methods were seen as a threat by other dentists and healers in Pergamum, because they wanted to get paid for their services. Their businesses were in jeopardy because the most successful healer in town was providing his services for free—and He was using the name of Jesus instead of one of the local gods. This angered the people, and a mob descended upon Antipas, dragged him to the temple of Serapis,[79] enclosed him in a bronze bull, and burned him alive as an act of worship to Serapis. Instead of compromising with the idol worshippers of Pergamum, Antipas was a model Christian who was faithful even to death.

---

[78] "Heiromartyr Antipas the Bishop of Pergamum and Disciple of St. John the Theologian," *Orthodox Church in America; http://oca.org/saints/ lives/2014/04/11/101052-hieromartyr-antipas-the-bishop-of-pergamum-and- disciple-of-st-jo* (accessed June 10, 2015).
[79] Mills, 71.

This was a significant event for the Christians at Pergamum who, in the midst of pressure to compromise with ritual feasts and sacrifices, had lost their bishop to martyrdom. In light of this event, Jesus praises their faithfulness to Him. They had remained true to His name, even when faced with the possibility of being martyred, like their bishop, for invoking His name.

## BALAAM AND BALAK

After encouraging the believers for their faithfulness, Jesus reprimands them for tolerating several heresies:

> *Nevertheless, I have a few things against you: There are some among you who hold to the teaching of Balaam, who taught Balak to entice the Israelites to sin so that they ate food sacrificed to idols and committed sexual immorality.* (Revelation 2:14).

The first heresy is the teaching of Balaam. This refers back to the Old Testament story of Balaam and Balak in Numbers 25. In short, the Moabite king Balak asked the seer Balaam to curse the Israelites. However, God would not allow Balaam to curse them. Since Balaam wanted the money Balak had offered him, Balaam advised Balak to entangle Israel with sexual immorality and idol worship. This would cause Israel to bring a curse down upon their own heads. In response to Balaam's teaching, Moabite women enticed Israelite men to have sexual relations with them and then invited them to the sacrifices of their gods, where the Israelite men ate the meat sacrificed to the idols and worshipped the false gods.[80]

---

[80] Fee, *Revelation*, 35.

By applying the story in Numbers to the believers at Pergamum, Jesus was saying that some of the Christians had compromised with idol worship and were headed down the same path as the ancient Israelites. This was not unique to the believers at Pergamum. We know from several other passages in the New Testament that there was some controversy over the temptation of Christians "to do what in itself was harmless, but which led to evil if it led to participation in pagan feasts"[81] (see Acts 15:29; 21:25; 1 Cor. 8).

A large part of the problem was the expectation in the ancient world that people would participate in idol worship as a normal part of society and business. If Christians refused to participate in the pagan feasts and rituals, they risked being ostracized from society, losing their livelihood, and even losing their citizenship. The believers had to decide whether they would participate in pagan feasts and sacrifices (which also involved temple prostitutes and sexual immorality) or whether they would hold to their Christian witness and risk ending up poor, persecuted, and possibly even dead.

> MODERN APPLICATION:
> We all face the temptation, in different ways, to compromise our faith in order to appease cultural expectations. In some cases, if we do not compromise, we risk losing relationships, business, reputation, etc. The example of Antipas reminds us of the importance of staying true to Christ, even when it costs us.

Antipas had remained faithful, and he had been martyred. Now the remaining believers had to choose. Many had remained faithful to Jesus, but some had gone the way of Balaam. They had *"loved the wages of unrighteousness"* (2 Pet. 2:15) and become

---

[81] Robertson, 306.

greedy for reward, just like Balaam (see Jude 11). These believers were participating in the idol worship and sexual immorality, but in their hearts they said, "But I'm still a follower of Christ." Yet Jesus bluntly reminds them of what happened with Balaam and the Israelites.

## NICOLAITANS, REPENT

Second, Jesus mentions the Nicolaitan heresy:

> *Likewise, you also have those who hold to the teaching of the Nicolaitans. Repent therefore! Otherwise, I will soon come to you and will fight against them with the sword of my mouth* (Revelation 2:15–16).

Unlike the believers at Ephesus, who rejected the Nicolaitan teaching, some of the Pergamum believers were following these false teachings related to authority and control. Considering that Pergamum was the government capital and a military city, it is not surprising that the believers here would have been tempted to take their cues from secular leaders and *"lord it over"* each other (Matt. 20:25). But Jesus made it clear that He does not endorse that type of leadership. When His disciples jockeyed for position, He told them,

> *Whoever wants to become great among you must be your servant, and whoever wants to be first must be your slave—just as the Son of Man did not come to be served, but to serve, and to give his life as a ransom for many* (Matthew 20:26–28).

Instead of dominating the people, the leaders of His Church should be gentle shepherds like Him, as the apostle Peter explains:

*Be shepherds of God's flock that is under your care, watching over them—not because you must, but because you are willing, as God wants you to be; not pursuing dishonest gain, but eager to serve; not lording it over those entrusted to you, but being examples to the flock (1 Peter 5:3).*

Jesus, the servant-hearted Great Shepherd, hates controlling and authoritarian leadership. Seeing that some of the believers in Pergamum were creating an oppressive

> MODERN APPLICATION:
> Jesus, the servant-hearted Great Shepherd, hates it when controlling and authoritarian leaders oppress His people.

hierarchy and seeking to dominate the people, He gives them an ultimatum: *"Repent therefore! Otherwise, I will soon come to you and will fight against them with the sword of my mouth"* (Rev. 2:16). In this verse, we see a division among the people. Jesus says, I will come to *you*, and I will fight against *them*. He is going to come to the church at Pergamum, and He is going to fight against those holding to the teaching of the Nicolaitans. This is why He changes the pronoun from *you* to *them*. His fight is not with the entire church but with those following this heresy. Gordon Fee sums it up like this:

This is not a battle against the whole church, although they are indeed to repent for letting this false teaching exist among them, but warfare carried on specifically "against them", the purveyors of and adherents to this false teaching.[82]

At the beginning of the letter, Jesus introduces Himself as the one with the double-edged sword, the one who has true authority. Here, in response to the abuse of authority, He threatens to use that sword.

## HIDDEN MANNA AND A WHITE STONE

Finally, Jesus ends the letter with this Messianic promise:

*Whoever has ears, let them hear what the Spirit says to the churches. To the one who is victorious, I will give some of the hidden manna. I will also give that person a white stone with a new name written on it, known only to the one who receives it* (Revelation 2:17).

The promise of hidden manna is the promise of a communion feast with Him—in direct contrast to the pagan ritual feasts. The entire letter revolves around this theme, this question of whether or not the believers will stay true to Christ and abstain from the pagan feasts and rituals. Thus, Jesus closes the letter by promising these rewards to those who are victorious and refuse, like Antipas, to sacrifice to idols.

A similar contrast between feasting with Christ and feasting in pagan worship is made by Paul in First Corinthians 10:14–22:

*Therefore, my dear friends, flee from idolatry. I speak to sensible people; judge for yourselves what I say. Is not the cup of thanksgiving for which we give thanks a*

---

[82] Fee, *Revelation*, 35.

*participation in the blood of Christ? And is not the bread that we break a participation in the body of Christ? Because there is one loaf, we, who are many, are one body, for we all share the one loaf. Consider the people of Israel: Do not those who eat the sacrifices participate in the altar? Do I mean then that food sacrificed to an idol is anything, or that an idol is anything? No, but the sacrifices of pagans are offered to demons, not to God, and I do not want you to be participants with demons. You cannot drink the cup of the Lord and the cup of demons too; you cannot have a part in both the Lord's table and the table of demons. Are we trying to arouse the Lord's jealousy? Are we stronger than he?*

Here, Paul compares the cup and table of the Lord with the cup and table of demons (the pagan feasts), declaring that Christians must not participate in both. His suggestion that doing so will arouse the Lord's jealousy shows that this pagan feasting is paramount to adultery in His eyes. Jesus also calls the believers to choose between the feasts of idols and the feast of Christ. He tells them they cannot participate in both, not really. If they think so, they are fooling themselves. But those who repent and shun the pagan feasts will be invited to feast with Christ.

Not only does the hidden manna symbolize a communion meal, but it is a metaphor for Jesus Himself. It speaks of union with Him. When the Jews asked Jesus for a sign that He had been sent from God, they referenced the manna God had sent to their ancestors as a sign from Heaven. *"What will you do?"* they asked (John 6:30). In response, Jesus said that the true bread from Heaven does not come from Moses but from God. And when the people asked for that bread, Jesus said, *"I am the bread of life. Whoever comes to me will never go hungry, and whoever believes in me will never be thirsty"* (John 6:35). In other words, He is the true manna from Heaven. To His faithful worshippers, He gives Himself.

Second, Jesus offers a white stone with the believer's name written on it. Many possible interpretations have been suggested for this stone. Two stand out prominently.

First, at that time in history, if a court jury found someone innocent, the individual received a white stone as proof of his or her acquittal. Second, white stones were also used as tickets to great public festivals.[83] Gorden Fee combines these two possibilities in this way:

> If one were to combine this evidence, the "hidden manna" they are to receive at Eschaton, vis-à-vis their refusal to participate in the local pagan festivals, represents their form of admission to the final festive meal that believers are to experience at the "marriage supper of the Lamb.[84]

Jesus is saying to the believers that if they chose not to participate in the pagan festivals, He declares them innocent (acquitted) and gives them a ticket to His bridal supper, where they will commune with Him. This supper is not just the Lord's Supper but also the marriage supper of Revelation 19. Because of their loyalty to Christ, these believers would be able to participate in this supper and receive the hidden manna and the white stone.

The final element to this Messianic promise is the new name, known only to the one who receives it, on the white

---

[83] Robertson, 307; Wright, 23.
[84] Fee, *Revelation*, 36.

stone. In the Bible, a person's name represents that person's character. So, when God renames a person, He is changing that person's identity. We see this with Abram, Sarai, Jacob, and Simon (also known as Abraham, Sarah, Israel, and Peter). The same principle applies to this new name that Jesus promises to those who participate in His marriage supper.[85] The Bride receives a new name when she marries her Husband. This new identity was very important and relevant to the believers at Pergamum, because refusing to participate in the pagan feasts essentially meant losing their identity within their society. They had lost membership in their trade guild, involvement in civic life, and their citizenship. In modern terms, it would be like the president of the United States demanding that all citizens worship him, and if they refuse, they lose their citizenship. Their social security numbers, birth certificates, driver's licenses, passports, and bank accounts would all be eliminated. They would be wiped from the system. That is what the Christians at Pergamum faced, and that is why the promise of a new identity was so meaningful.

Jesus is essentially promising them the same reality Paul talks about in Philippians 3:15–20, where he paints a contrast between those who claim the name of Christ but live as His enemies by participating in pagan worship and those who are true followers of Christ and find their citizenship in Heaven:

*All of us, then, who are mature should take such a view of things. And if on some point you think differently, that too God will make clear to you. Only let us live up to what we have already attained. Join together in following my*

---

[85] Hendricksen, 69.

*example, brothers and sisters, and just as you have us as a model, keep your eyes on those who live as we do. For, as I have often told you before and now tell you again even with tears, many live as enemies of the cross of Christ. Their destiny is destruction, their god is their stomach, and their glory is in their shame. Their mind is set on earthly things. But our citizenship is in heaven. And we eagerly await a Savior from there, the Lord Jesus Christ* (Philippians 3:15–20).

The white stone with a new name on it is Jesus' offer of a new citizenship to those who have abandoned their earthly citizenship in order to follow Him. Not only are they innocent, but they have a new citizenship and a new identity as His Bride. This new identity is placed on a white stone, just as in the ancient world important declarations would be inscribed on white stones and then mounted on a dark stone as a placard. Jesus is saying that their new identity and citizenship is an important declaration, because they are important and valuable people— citizens of His enduring Kingdom.

This new identity is known only to the one who receives it— not in the sense of secrecy but of ownership. This phrase comes from a Hebrew idiom that connects the word *know* with the idea of ownership or something that is experienced only by that individual. So, the more accurate translation of this phrase is "owned only by the one who receives it." It is not a secret name, but it does belong to each individual exclusively.[86] This speaks of intimacy. Each individual will personally experience their own new identity as one who is united with Christ.

---

[86] Chilton, 111.

# THYATIRA–TRADE GUILDS

# seven

Southeast of Pergamum, about fifty miles toward the center of modern Turkey, is Thyatira, the fourth of the seven cities. Though in the ancient world Thyatira was not an important or well-known city, it receives the longest letter from Jesus.[87] This is, at least in part, due to the Hebrew Chiastic Arch form, in which the middle item in a list would have the greatest emphasis.[88] Founded as a military outpost of Pergamum, Thyatira sat in a valley between two other valleys and was, therefore, vulnerable to attack. Because of this, a Roman garrison was stationed there, not only to protect Thyatira but also to prevent attack against the nearby capital of Pergamum.[89]

As an easily accessible city that people continually traveled through, Thyatira became a trade city where those who worked

---

[87] Gregg, 70; Mills, 57.
[88] We will look at the significance of the Chiastic Arch in more detail in Chapter 11.
[89] Hendriksen, 71–72.

in various trades (such as wool-workers, linen-workers, makers of outer garments, dyers, leather-workers, tanners, potters) gathered in order to sell their goods and perform their services. Thyatira became especially known for its purple dye industry and its copper and bronze workers.[90] Lydia, the dealer in purple cloth mentioned in Acts 16:14, was from Thyatira.

At that time in history, the workers in these various industries all belonged to trade guilds, which could be compared to our modern unions. Each of these guilds had a deity, and being part of a guild meant worshipping the guild deity. This was a huge problem for the Christians who worked in these industries. William Hendriksen summarizes the difficulty:

> The situation, therefore, was somewhat as follows: if you wish to get ahead in this world, you must belong to a guild; if you belong to a guild, your very membership implies that you worship its god. You will be expected to attend the guild festivals and to eat food part of which is offered to the tutelary deity and which you receive on your table as a gift from the god. And then, when the feast ends, and the real—grossly immoral—fun begins, you must not walk out unless you desire to become the object of ridicule and persecution!

> In this difficult situation what must a Christian do? If he quits the union, he loses his position and his standing in society. He may have to suffer want, hunger, and persecution. On the other hand, if he remains in the guild and attends the immoral feasts, eating things

---

[90] Wright, 25; Robertson, 308.

sacrificed to idols and committing fornications, he denies his Lord.[91]

Because of this, many people chose to leave their guilds when they became Christians, which was the equivalent of losing their jobs. The Christians in Thyatira faced the same dilemma as those in Pergamum, only more so, because the trade guilds were such a significant part of the town. To the believers in this situation, Jesus writes a letter that would have both comforted and challenged them.

## EYES OF FIRE, FEET OF BRONZE

Jesus begins with a description of Himself that directly challenges the local deities of Thyatira: *"To the angel of the church in Thyatira write: These are the words of the Son of God, whose eyes are like blazing fire and whose feet are like burnished bronze"* (Rev. 2:18). This would have resonated with the Thyatira Christians on several levels.

First, the local guardian deity of the city was Apollo Tyrimnaeus, the god of the bronze trade. Apollo was the son of Zeus (the chief god in Greek mythology), and the local coins carried his image with the inscription, "son of god." In Jesus' self-description, *"blazing fire"* and *"burnished bronze"* are clear references to the bronze trade. Through them, Jesus is saying, "I am greater than this so-called god of bronze. I am the true son of God."[92]

Second, worship of Apollo Tyrimnaeus was mixed with the Emperor cult's worship of Caesar, who was also believed to be

[91] Hendriksen, 71–72.
[92] Wright, 25.

the incarnate son of God. Because of this, images of Caesar were carved into walls and pillars throughout Thyatira. Statues and images of the Roman emperors and their families were sometimes carved with bare feet to indicate that they had "entered the realm of the divine."[93] Thus, by appearing barefoot, Jesus declares Himself the true (and only) son of God. This is the only place in Revelation where Jesus is explicitly called the "son of God," and it stands in direct opposition to the claims of the Imperial cult.[94]

To the Christians who were leaving their trade guilds in order to stay true to their faith, Jesus sends this reassurance that He is the true son of God, superior to the local trade gods and the Caesar. He says, "I am the real Son of God. I am greater than the trade deity. I am greater than the fire and the metalworkers. I am greater than all these things."

## JEZEBEL TOLERATED

After this introduction, Jesus briefly praises the church, saying, "I know your deeds, your love and faith, your service and perseverance, and that you are now doing more than you did at first" (Rev. 2:19). This is a strong commendation. So much is right about the church in Thyatira, yet a serious heresy lurks in their midst. For this reason, Jesus follows His praise with a strong rebuke:

*Nevertheless, I have this against you: You tolerate that woman Jezebel, who calls herself a prophet. By her teaching*

---

[93] Wilson, *Revelation*, 27.
[94] Chilton, 112.

> *she misleads my servants into sexual immorality and the eating of food sacrificed to idols* (Revelation 2:20).

This woman Jesus referred to as Jezebel probably was not actually named Jezebel. Instead, *Jezebel* is synonymous with idolatry and immorality. Only one woman in the history of Israel had killed the prophets. She and her husband Ahab were the first to lead the people of Israel into wholesale worship of other gods. The Christians would have recognized that Jesus was saying this woman was acting like the Jezebel of the Old Testament, who had led people away from the one true God and into pagan idolatry (see 1 Kings 16:31; 18:4, 13, 19; 19:1–2).

Jesus calls her Jezebel because of her character and because she was leading people into compromise, probably teaching something along the lines of syncretism (a blending of religions). She was telling the Christians to compromise with the pagan culture and religion, suggesting they could stay in the trade guilds and participate in the rituals while being "Christian" in their hearts.

This would have enabled the believers to avoid persecution—"one could

> MODERN APPLICATION:
> Unwillingness to suffer persecution for Christ will lead to compromise.

be a part of the believing community in Thyatira without losing one's friends and (especially) one's position in the trade guilds."[95] But Jesus, who identifies Himself as the one with eyes like blazing fire, sees the selfish motives of the people's hearts. "His penetrating eyes see the hidden motive that makes people follow Jezebel, namely, unwillingness to suffer persecution for the sake of Christ."[96]

[95] Fee, *Revelation*, 39.
[96] Hendriksen, 71–72.

Later in the letter, we learn that Jezebel also advocated learning *"Satan's so-called deep secrets"* (Rev. 2:24). Hendriksen suggests this refers to a teaching that actually painted participation in pagan festivals as a positive for Christians. This removed the dilemma they faced with the trade guilds:

> In this difficult situation the prophetess Jezebel pretended to know the real solution to the problem, the way out of the difficulty. She, apparently, argued thus: in order to conquer Satan, you must know him. You will never be able to conquer sin unless you have become thoroughly acquainted with it by experience. In brief, a Christian should learn to know "the deep things of Satan". By all means attend the guild-feasts and commit fornication... and still remain a Christian; nay rather, become a better Christian![97]

This was the danger of allowing Jezebel to exist, unchecked, in their midst. And that is exactly what the leaders of the church at Thyatira had done. Because they had not rebuked her, some of the Christians were being deceived by her teaching. Though the church as a whole had not capitulated to her false teaching, they had allowed it to continue. They were "virtually tolerating a heathen prophetess and thus allowing her pernicious influences to damage many."[98] This was a serious error and danger to the church in that city, and because of this, Jesus announces next that He is taking matters into His own hands.

---

[97] Hendriksen, 71–72.
[98] Terry, 303.

# A BED OF SUFFERING

The letter continues:

> *I have given her time to repent of her immorality, but she is unwilling. So I will cast her on a bed of suffering, and I will make those who commit adultery with her suffer intensely, unless they repent of her ways. I will strike her children dead. Then all the churches will know that I am he who searches hearts and minds, and I will repay each of you according to your deeds* (Revelation 2:21–23).

First, we see that Jesus had warned this woman and given her time to repent, but she chose not to. She purposefully refused the conviction of the Spirit and instead embraced the agenda of the enemy. Jesus, whose heart is for every individual, tries to rescue the woman from her deception, but she is unwilling. It's important to recognize here that she (not Jesus) was the one who was unwilling.

MODERN APPLICATION: Because of His great love for every person, Jesus always tries to rescue people from deception. No matter what a person has done, He is willing to forgive and redeem, if they are willing to come to Him. When people embrace spiritual darkness, it is because they were unwilling to turn to Christ (not because He was unwilling to have them).

Because she is unwilling to repent, Jesus prophesies two punishments. He says He will cast her on a bed of suffering and strike her children dead. This sounds horrible to our modern ears if we do not understand it in its cultural context. Wilson describes the significance of the first punishment:

"Bed" (Gk. *kline*) can also be translated as "couch." It is thus used ironically to describe Jezebel and her followers, who reclined on marble couches while dining in the banqueting hall of the pagan temples. Such couches were also used for sexual immorality, as depicted in Greek vase paintings and described in Greek literature. Because Jezebel had used her freedom to lie on a couch of pleasure in the temples, God would instead make it a bed of sickness unless she repented.[99]

Jezebel and her followers had chosen to worship false gods; the result would be sickness and suffering. This is reminiscent of Jesus' statement:

> *If anyone causes one of these little ones—those who believe in me—to stumble, it would be better for them to have a large millstone hung around their neck and to be drowned in the depths of the sea* (Matthew 18:6).

Leading other believers astray is a serious offense against the great Shepherd of the sheep. As we see in this passage, Jesus will fight to protect His followers from deception and destructive false teachings.

Second, from Old Testament imagery we know *"her children"* is a reference to her followers, not her literal children (see Isa. 57:3).[100] Jesus is not threatening to kill Jezebel's literal children; He is warning her followers of the grave danger they are in if they continue to follow her teaching.[101] He is also warning Jezebel of

---

[99] Wilson, *Revelation*, 27–28.
[100] Chilton, 115.
[101] "The killing *of her children with death* is, perhaps, another allusion to the history of Jezebel in the slaughter of the false prophet." Terry, 303.

what will come of the heritage she is creating through this false teaching. This is the same prophecy that Queen Jezebel received (see 1 Kings 21:21). Because she had led God's people into idolatry and immorality, God said He would cut off her inheritance and destiny. In the culture of that day, having children to carry on one's name was a very big deal. It was how a person's memory and impact continued on after that person had died. In light of that, what Jesus is saying to this woman is: "If you continue in this way, you will be cut off. Your heritage will not continue on." He would not allow her heresy to continue.

The irony, here, is that Jezebel and her followers were attempting to save their lives instead of losing them. This is the opposite of what Jesus said to do: *"For whoever wants to save their life will lose it, but whoever loses their life for me will find it"* (Matt. 16:25). So, to those who were compromising in an effort to protect their lives from persecution, Jesus says such actions will actually cause them to lose their inheritance. This is quite ironic.

We see the severity of the issue in the progression of the pronouns:

> What began as "unless *they* repent of *her* ways" is then
> followed with "*all the churches* will know", which in turn
> is followed by "I will repay each of *you* according to *your*
> deeds."[102]

If Jezebel's followers didn't repent of their idolatry and immorality, Jesus would make them an example to all the churches. If they chose the way of destruction, He would use

---

[102] Fee, *Revelation*, 41.

their story as a warning to others. And He promises that the people in the church at Thyatira would be repaid for their deeds, individually, whether good or evil. This may seem harsh, but the whole purpose of these letters was to warn the believers of the coming Roman armies and destruction connected to AD 70. In that context, He wants His followers to know that those who are compromising will not be protected. They will find themselves numbered among those who had refused to repent of their evil deeds, including worshiping demons and idols and committing sexual immorality (see Rev. 9:20–21).

## HOLD ON TO WHAT YOU HAVE

After His strong warning to Jezebel and her followers, Jesus says to the remainder of the church:

> Now I say to the rest of you in Thyatira, to you who do not hold to her teaching and have not learned Satan's so-called deep secrets, "I will not impose any other burden on you, except to hold on to what you have until I come" (Revelation 2:24–25).

Here we find Jesus' mention of the deep things of Satan. The text is not clear whether, as Hendriksen suggested,[103] Jezebel used this terminology herself or whether it was Jesus' assessment of her teachings. Fee suggests that Jezebel may have been promoting her teaching as "the deep things of God" but that Christ was accurately renaming it "the deep things of Satan."[104] Either way, it's clear that her teachings were demonic

---

[103] Hendriksen, 71–72.
[104] Fee, *Revelation*, 42.

and were bringing great harm to some believers in the church in Thyatira.

Because of the seriousness of the issue, this is one of the rare places where a New Testament writer uses the name of an Old Testament character to refer to an ungodly mindset or spirit. The Jezebel spirit does not just promote sexual immorality (though it may involve it); at its core, the Jezebel spirit has to do with compromise. This can relate to any area of faith. In Thyatira we find a stark picture of this struggle in the church between compromising with the trade guilds and remaining true to the faith. Though the issues are different in modern Christianity, the temptation to compromise some area of our faith is just as real.

Jesus' rebuke of Jezebel and her followers comes between two commendations of the church at Thyatira as a whole. He begins by praising them. Then He inserts His judgment of Jezebel. Then He ends by praising the church again, telling them that as long as they don't follow Jezebel, they are doing well. He has no other rule or obligation for them. Essentially He says, "If you're not following Jezebel, just stay on the path you're on, because it's the right path.

## AUTHORITY OVER THE NATIONS

Jesus ends His letter to Thyatira with this Messianic promise for the faithful ones:

> *To the one who is victorious and does my will to the end, I will give authority over the nations—that one "will rule them with an iron scepter and will dash them to pieces*

*like pottery"—just as I have received authority from my Father. I will also give that one the morning star. Whoever has ears, let them hear what the Spirit says to the churches* (Revelation 2:26–29).

This promise of authority over the nations is a direct reference to Psalm 2,[105] one of the great Messianic psalms:

*Ask me, and I will make the nations your inheritance, the ends of the earth your possession. You will break them with a rod of iron; you will dash them to pieces like pottery* (Psalm 2:8–9).

As a trade guild city, Thyatira would have been closely acquainted with the arts of metal working and pottery. A great deal of metal and clay items were both made and sold there. Thus, when Jesus talks of ruling with an iron scepter and dashing the nations to pieces like pottery, He uses very vivid images for the Christians of Thyatira. Though these materials were household items throughout the ancient world, in Thyatira, many of the Christians would have had personal experience with those trades or been intimately acquainted with someone who did. It was part of the city's DNA, and it was especially relevant and meaningful to them.

Not only does Jesus declare that He, as the Messiah, has authority over the nations, but He promises to give that authority to His faithful followers. He is not boasting; He is declaring His authority. And He promises to share that authority with His people!

---

[105] Fee, *Revelation*, 42.

## THE MORNING STAR

Jesus continues, *"I will also give that one the morning star"* (Rev. 2:28). The morning star was probably a reference to the planet Venus, which shines most brightly in early morning. This star was a sign of authority: "From Babylonian times, it was a symbol of rule. The Roman legions carried Venus's zodiac sign, the bull, on their standards."[106] In other words, the promise of the morning star is an echo of Jesus' first promise to give them authority over the nations. The two symbols are one and the same.

Later in Revelation, Jesus identifies Himself as the true morning star: *"I, Jesus, have sent my angel to give you this testimony for the churches. I am the Root and the Offspring of David, and the bright Morning Star"* (Rev. 22:16). Jesus had received the promise of authority over the nations that was originally delivered to His ancestor, King David (see Matt. 3:17; Acts 13:33). He had become the true Son of David, the King who would perpetuate David's house forever in the new covenant Kingdom. Thus, He is the bright Morning Star, the forever ruler over all.

Prior to the end of the old covenant in AD 70, the light of Christ was partially hidden. It was veiled and needed to be unveiled. We get this sense in Peter's mention of the morning star, which he prophesied would rise in the believers' hearts:

*We also have the prophetic message as something completely reliable, and you will do well to pay attention to it, as to a light shining in a dark place, until the day dawns and the morning star rises in your hearts* (2 Peter 1:19).

---

[106] Wilson, *Revelation*, 28.

When Peter wrote this, the gospel was a light shining in a dark place, but a light obscured in part by the old covenant veil (see 2 Cor. 3). However, he looked forward to the dawn of the coming day, when the morning star would rise in believers' hearts and be unveiled to the world. This is not a reference to eternity but to the full revelation of Christ and His new covenant following the AD 70 destruction of Jerusalem. Thus, Jesus' promise of the morning star is a promise of Himself as the ruling King. It is a promise of the new covenant reign and "a sign of the special vocation of Christians"[107] as lights and spiritual authorities in this world. Or, as Gordon Fee puts it, "The victors will be given eschatological glory, which they will share with Christ himself."[108] It is not unlike the promise Jesus gave His disciples:

> *You are those who have stood by me in my trials. And I confer on you a kingdom, just as my Father conferred one on me, so that you may eat and drink at my table in my kingdom and sit on thrones, judging the twelve tribes of Israel* (Luke 22:28–30).

To His followers who had stood by Him in persecution, Jesus promises authority to rule and judge the nations (see also 1 Cor. 6:2). He commissions them to help usher in His new covenant reign of peace and love on earth.

---

[107] Wright, 27.
[108] Fee, *Revelation*, 42.

# eight

# SARDIS–SLEEPING CITY

The fifth city along the route is Sardis, a spectacular city situated in the Hermes Valley and renowned for its wealth. With goldmines nearby, Sardis was the first city to mint gold and silver coins, and because of this, it became so affluent that its name was a sort of byword for wealth. The goldmines upstream caused the River Pactolus, which ran through the city, to flow with gold dust.[109] According to Greek mythology, King Midas had cured himself of his magical golden touch by bathing in this river, causing the river to run with gold dust.[110] This is why Gordon Fee writes of Sardis, "The city also presents us with an interesting paradox, since its history and significance were both real and illusory."[111]

---

[109] Mills, 77.

[110] Joshua J. Mark, "Croesus," *Ancient History Encyclopedia* (Sept. 2, 2009); http://www.ancient.eu/croesus/ (accessed July 15, 2015).

[111] Fee, *Revelation*, 44.

Sardis' most famous king, Croesus, who ruled from 560 to 547 BC, was legendary for his wealth. During his reign, Sardis was the capitol of Lydia (modern Turkey). Croesus financed the great Temple of Artemis in Ephesus that was one of the Seven Wonders of the Ancient World. He also began a temple to Artemis in Sardis, but that temple was never completed. Under his rule, the city flourished. It had everything a city could want: "choice location, climate, wealth and culture."[112] Because of this, the people of Sardis became overly confident in their security.

Sardis was set atop a hill with sheer cliffs all around. These cliffs are at near 90 degree angles and incredibly difficult to climb. The only normal way of access was along a narrow piece of land to the south, and this was fortified to prevent attack. The city was considered, by many, to be impregnable.[113] Because of the geography, Sardis was more fortified than most other cities in that area. Yet in 549 BC, Cyrus the Great, king of Persia, captured the city using skilled soldier-climbers who scaled the walls and attacked Sardis in the middle of the night. The city was caught completely off guard and demolished. It was then absorbed into Cyrus' kingdom, becoming the westernmost city of the Persian Empire. Years later, in 218 BC, the city was once again caught off guard and captured by soldier-climbers employed by the Greek king Antiochus the Great.[114]

Over the years, the original city of Sardis was gradually abandoned because the hill was too small for a growing city, and a new city formed on a lower plain nearby.[115] Then, in AD 17, a major earthquake ripped through the region and brought

---

[112] Fee, *Revelation*, 44.
[113] Hendriksen, 73.
[114] Ibid.
[115] Ibid.

sudden destruction to Sardis again. In John's day, in the wake of this third sudden destruction, "Sardis was facing decay, a slow but sure death."[116] Sardis was a city of great wealth, which brought a sense of stability to its citizens, yet it also had a history of being suddenly overtaken or destroyed. In Sardis, great wealth and comfort were undergirded by a subtle insecurity.

Despite this, because of its location, climate, and tremendous wealth, Sardis enjoyed a position of significance. It was a crossroads for trade and a place of culture. Unlike Thyatira, which was filled primarily with common people in trade guilds, Sardis was filled with wealthy nobles and the upper class of that region. It was a preeminent city in that region from approximately 700 BC until AD 700.

## THE JEWISH PRESENCE

Before getting to the details of Jesus' letter to the church at Sardis, it's important to note the large Jewish presence in Sardis. Compared to other cities in that area, Sardis had an enormous Jewish population dating back hundreds of years. In *Antiquities,* Josephus tells us about how so many Jews landed in this area. This is an excerpt from a letter from one king to another king in the sixth century BC:

> Here is my greeting: If you are in good health, it is well. I am also in sound health. Learning that the people in Lydia and Phrygia are revolting, I have come to consider this as requiring very serious attention on my part. On taking counsel with my friends as to what to be done,

---

[116] Ibid.

I determined to transport 2,000 Jewish families with their effects from Mesopotamia and Babylonia to the fortresses and most important places for I am convinced that they will be loyal guardians of our interests because of their piety to God.[117]

The people in this region were revolting, and the king's solution to this problem was to import two thousand Jewish families. He believed them to be such good people and good followers of their God that they would bring peace to the area. The letter continues:

I am convinced that they will be loyal guardians of our interests because of their piety to God. I know that they have had the testimony of their forefathers to their good faith and eagerness to do as they are asked. It is my will, therefore, though it may be a troublesome matter, that they should be transported. Since I have promised it, we will use their own laws. And when you have brought them to the places mentioned you shall give to each of them a place to build a house, land to cultivate and plant with vines, and shall exempt them from the payment of taxes from the produce of the soil for the first ten years. And also, until they get produce from the soil, let them have grain measured out to them for feeding their servants, and let there be given also those engaged in public service sufficient for their needs in order that though receiving kind treatment from us they may show themselves the more eager in our cause and take as much thought for their nation as possible that it may not be molested by anyone.[118]

---

[117] Josephus, *Antiquities*, book 12, chapter 3, section 4.
[118] Ibid.

This importation of Jews to Sardis and the surrounding area during the Persian Empire was prophesied in Obadiah 1:20–21:

*This company of Israelite exiles who are in Canaan will possess the land as far as Zarephath; the exiles from Jerusalem who are in Sepharad [Sardis[119]] will possess the towns of the Negev. Deliverers will go up on Mount Zion to govern the mountains of Esau. And the kingdom will be the Lord's.*

In the Babylonian exile, the Jews were scattered throughout the empire. To our knowledge, Esther was never in Sardis, but Sardis was the westernmost city of the Persian Empire while she was queen. Thus, her brave defense of the Jews against Haman's decree protected the Jews in Sardis, who had been there since as early as the sixth century BC. This is how Sardis of the first century came to have such a large Jewish population.

What this meant for the gospel was that, as the apostles traveled and preached, they encountered groups of Jews that had been dispersed around the known world. These Jews already had a foundation in God's Word, and their neighbors were already familiar with the God of the Jews. This created an important inroad for the preaching of the gospel, not just in Israel but throughout the known world of that time. When the apostles came, the framework for the gospel was often already in place, and they simply needed to explain that the Messiah had come. It is amazing to see how God used the Jewish dispersion to usher in the new covenant among the gentiles. Their calling as a nation, after all, was to be a light to the world and to show the gentile nations what God is like.

---

[119] Sepharad was an ancient name for Sardis. Wilson, *Biblical Turkey*, 309.

The gospel had taken root at Sardis, where the Jewish framework must have been strong. Yet something was wrong. This is the main subject of Jesus' letter to that church.

## SEVEN SPIRITS, SEVEN STARS

Jesus begins His letter to Sardis with this self-description: *"To the angel of the church in Sardis write: These are the words of him who holds the seven spirits of God and the seven stars"* (Rev. 3:1).[120] This introduction is much more mystical than the introduction to the other letters. Here, Jesus is presenting Himself as a very spiritual, cosmic, mystical, in-the-spirit Jesus. As such, He can discern the spiritual climate of their hearts. He sees past the natural into the spiritual realm, and thus, He sees what is truly going on with the Christians at Sardis. This is significant to the church at Sardis because, as we will soon learn, how they appeared in the natural was not how they really were in the spirit.

## SPIRITUALLY DEAD

Immediately after His introduction, Jesus addresses what's really going on at Sardis:

> *I know your deeds; you have a reputation of being alive, but you are dead. Wake up! Strengthen what remains and is about to die, for I have found your deeds unfinished in the sight of my God.* (Revelation 3:1–2).

---

[120] The *"seven spirits of God"* is likely a reference to the seven spirits of God listed in Isaiah 11, which is to say, seven attributes of the Holy Spirit.

They had form without power. They appeared to be spiritual; they appeared to be alive, but their hearts were really dead. Their great wealth and comfort had caused them to deaden their senses spiritually. While many other Christians faced persecution, the Christians of Sardis were getting along comfortably. In fact, we might conjecture that it was because of their spiritual deadness that they faced no persecution, despite the large Jewish population. The Christians in Sardis were not much of a spiritual threat, so there was not much reason to persecute them. The Sardinian Christians looked like Christians, but they were not operating in supernatural power. Their senses were dulled; they believed they were OK and had everything they needed. So, the mystical and spiritual Jesus reminds them that He sees into their hearts. He knows what's really going on, and He is warning them of what is coming their way.

Jesus then tells them to *"Wake up!"* Actually, a better translation of this phrase is: *"Become watchful!"* While *wake up* implies they are asleep, *be watchful* speaks to alertness. The sense of the original language is "You are awake but not alert or watchful." So, He is telling them to snap out of their spiritual haze and dullness of senses so they can become aware of what is going on in the spirit. If they are only living by their natural senses, they will miss the important warnings coming their way. And they will be caught up in the AD 70 destruction.

Then Jesus tells them to *"strengthen what remains and is about to die."* This is a play on words, as the name *Sardis* means "the remains."[121] He is saying that, just as the natural city was in decline, so the spiritual climate of the church was in decline. It was about to die, unless the believers strengthened what was left,

---

[121] Nee, 53.

> MODERN APPLICATION:
> As believers, the way we live should impact the community around us.

unless they revived themselves spiritually. As it was, their deeds were unfinished, which may be Jesus' tactful way of saying that the way they were living out the gospel had left a lot to be desired. Thus, He calls them to return "to a steadfastness toward the gospel in their complacent city."[122] It wasn't enough for them to be Christian in an outward manner of form without power. They needed to be spiritually awake and alive.

## LIKE A THIEF IN THE NIGHT

The believers of Sardis were quite unaware of their desperate situation, clueless about the real threat that stood on the horizon in the form of the Roman army. In light of this, Jesus continues:

> *Remember, therefore, what you have received and heard; hold it fast, and repent. But if you do not wake up, I will come like a thief, and you will not know at what time I will come to you* (Revelation 3:3).

What they had received and heard was not only the gospel but also Jesus' warnings about the coming tribulation in Matthew 24. This included a mandate to keep watch: "*Therefore keep watch, because you do not know on what day your Lord will come*" (Matt. 24:42). However, the believers at Sardis had become comfortable and complacent. They had stopped watching. As a result, they were in danger of being unprepared for the day of the Lord, for Christ's coming in judgment upon Jerusalem, which

---

[122] Fee, *Revelation*, 47.

also affected all Jewish communities throughout the Roman Empire. In the history of their city, they had twice succumbed to attack due to this very sort of confident complacency. That arrogant belief, "We are safe. No one can harm us. We can just relax in our wealth and comfort," had been their downfall. "The parallel with the church's lack of vigilance, and its need to wake up lest it fall under judgment is striking."[123]

Sardis was an incredibly fortified city; if they had just maintained watch, they never would have been overthrown. N.T. Wright describes this attitude and their subsequent downfall well:

The city had been thought, for a long time, completely impregnable. It was secure, sitting on top of its steep hill. Attackers might come and go, but the citizens were quite content to see them do so. They knew they could never be captured.

Until one night, during the reign of the famous King Croesus, the invading Persian army found a way in. Someone, greatly daring, got up part of the sheer cliff and managed a surprise attack. Because nobody was expecting it, the result was all the more devastating.[124]

The citizens of Sardis had become over-confident and lazy—not just once, but twice. As a result, as Hendriksen says:

Again and again, the self-satisfied and boastful inhabitants of Sardis had seen destruction coming

---

[123] Beasley-Murray, 94, 120.
[124] Wright, 29.

upon them "as a thief in the night," most suddenly and unexpectedly.[125]

This is what Jesus alludes to when He talks about coming to them as a *"thief in the night."* Because of their history, the believers of Sardis would have found this warning especially poignant. The apostle Paul had warned of this reality, too: *"For you know very well that the day of the Lord will come like a thief in the night"* (1 Thess. 5:2). The exact time of the impending destruction was not known, but it was near, and therefore, the first century Christians needed to be on constant watch. This was the danger of the cavalier attitude at Sardis:

> If this continues, the church in Sardis will suffer the same fate as the city had suffered six hundred centuries earlier. Jesus 'will come like a thief' (verse 3), and they won't know what time it will happen. This echoes similar sayings in Paul and Peter, and in the teachings of Jesus himself (1 Thessalonians 5.2; 2 Peter 3.10; Matthew 24.43). It was obviously a regular warning note sounded among the early Christians.[126]

In Matthew 24, Jesus had told them the signs of His coming, but they would only recognize those signs if they were alert and watchful.

It is important to add here that Jesus' prophecy was specific to that time in history, leading up to the destruction of Jerusalem in AD 70. Jesus' declaration to the believers at Sardis, *"I will come to you,"* indicates a clear audience (Sardis) and timeframe (AD 70). It is not a prophecy of a time in the future when Jesus will

---

[125] Hendriksen, 73.
[126] Wright, 30.

come and snatch believers up to Heaven in a secret rapture. Though this is widely taught in futurist camps, it is far from the historical biblical context. As David Chilton says, "The failure of commentators and

> MODERN APPLICATION:
> Jesus is not coming like "a thief in the night" in our future. We do not need to watch for a secret rapture, as this was about Jesus' coming in judgment in AD 70.

preachers to understand this simple fact is the predictable result of a flat, futurist hermeneutic bordering on Biblical illiteracy."[127] The only proper understanding of this is in its historical context.

## WHITE GARMENTS

After His strong warning to the complacent Christians of Sardis, Jesus gives two Messianic promises to those who remain faithful to Him. First, He says:

> *Yet you have a few people in Sardis who have not soiled their clothes. They will walk with me, dressed in white, for they are worthy. The one who is victorious will, like them, be dressed in white* (Revelation 3:4–5).

The fact that believers will wear white garments is mentioned frequently in the Book of Revelation (see Rev. 3:18; 4:4; 6:11; 7:9, 13; 19:14), but it had special relevance in Sardis, because they were famous for wearing a certain type of red garment.[128] In contrast to the usual garb of their city, Jesus says they will "wear white robes, as people did in triumphal processions, and as the newly baptized would do when they emerged from the water."[129]

---

[127] Chilton, 121.
[128] Gregg, 74.
[129] Wright, 31.

As a city with a history of loyalty to Rome, the citizens of Sardis would have been familiar with Roman triumphal processions, and most likely they would have participated in them. As the returning heroes marched through the city, the citizens would have donned white clothing and lined the streets to honor the victorious warriors. "In like manner some in Sardis will be considered worthy to join in the Lord's triumph when he returns as conqueror."[130] We see this in the victory march described in the apocalyptic imagery of Revelation: *"The armies of heaven were following him, riding on white horses and dressed in fine linen, white and clean"* (Rev. 19:14). The faithful ones will be worthy to walk with Christ in His victory parade, just as the apostle Paul said: *"But thanks be to God, who always leads us in triumph in Christ"* (2 Cor. 1:14 NASB; see also Col. 2:14).

Not only do the white garments symbolize victory and honor, but they also symbolize the recreation experienced in the new birth. The old person dies, and the new person is born clothed with Christ (see Gal. 3:27; Eph. 4:24; Col. 3:10). David Chilton summarizes it like this:

> Our being clothed in the white clothes of righteousness, therefore, takes place *definitively* at our baptism (Gal. 3:27), progressively as we work out our salvation in daily obedience to God's commandments, "putting on" the Christian graces and virtues (Col. 3:5–17), and *finally* at the Last Day (Col. 3:4; Jude 24).[131]

In both senses, then, the white robes symbolize the believer's victorious new life and participation with Christ in His victory over sin and death.

---

[130] Fee, *Revelation*, 48.
[131] Chilton, 122.

# NAMES IN THE BOOK OF LIFE

Second, Jesus promises:

> *I will never blot out the name of that person from the book of life, but will acknowledge that name before my Father and his angels. Whoever has ears, let them hear what the Spirit says to the churches* (Revelation 3:5–6).

Here, Jesus promises eternal salvation to His faithful followers. Implied in this promise is the possibility that believers can walk away from Christ and, as a result, have their names erased from the book of life.[132] The idea that one can be blotted out of God's book dates back to Exodus 32:32–33, where God tells Moses, *"Whoever has sinned against me I will blot out of my book."*[133] In Psalm 69:28, David calls it "the book of life," praying that his enemies will be *"be blotted out of the book of life and not be listed with the righteous."* Paul uses this same term in his commendation of several of his co-laborers, *"whose names are in the book of life"* (Phil. 4:3).

In the first century, many cities, including Sardis, had an official register that listed the names of all the male citizens. If a citizen was condemned for a crime, the city authorities would first blot his name from the book (removing his citizenship) so that the death sentence could be fulfilled without damaging the city's reputation.[134] In this way, they essentially said, "This person is not one of us." Evidence of this practice is found in Dio Chrysostom:

---

[132] In other words, this verse directly contradicts the traditional Calvinist teaching of the perseverance of the saints, or "once saved, always saved." Mills, 81.
[133] Wright, 31.
[134] Wright, 31; Wilson, *Biblical Turkey*, 310.

And so I now wish to tell you of a practice which I know is followed at Athens, and here too, I imagine, in accordance with a most excellent law. In Athens, for instance, whenever any citizen has to suffer death at the hands of the state for his crime, his name is erased first. Why is this done? One reason is that he may no longer be considered a citizen when he undergoes such a punishment but, so far as that is possible, as having become an alien. Then too I presume that it is looked upon as not the least part of the punishment itself, that even the appellation should no longer be seen of the man who had gone so far in wickedness, but should be utterly blotted out, just as, I believe traitors are denied burial, so that in the future there may be no trace whatever of a wicked man.[135]

Milton Terry connects this promise, *"I will never blot out the name of that person from the book of life,"* with Jesus' promise to the church at Smyrna—*"The one who is victorious will not be hurt at all by the second death"* (Rev. 2:11). True followers of Christ, true citizens of His eternal Kingdom, will live with Him forever.[136] Because they are not convicted, but instead forgiven, they are not put to death, and their names are not erased from the book of life.

By using this imagery, Jesus speaks to the Christians of Sardis about the Old Testament reality of the book of life, but in a modern and relatable context. And once again, He reassures His faithful followers that though the world may reject and persecute them, they are citizens of His eternal Kingdom. If the

---

[135] Dio Chrysostom, *Orations* 31:84; quoted in Wilson, *Biblical Turkey*, 310.
[136] Terry, 306.

Christians in Sardis followed His advice to wake up spiritually, they probably would experience some persecution. They might lose their citizenship in Sardis as a result, but they would not lose their citizenship in Heaven.

# PHILADELPHIA—
# EARTHQUAKE TOWN

The sixth city, Philadelphia, is twenty-five miles southeast of Sardis, in the Hermes Valley. Built in the second century BC, Philadelphia was the youngest of the seven cities of Revelation. The modern name for this city is Alaşehir, meaning "the city of God," and it is home to about 110,000 people. Because the modern city was built right on top of the ancient city, excavation of the ancient sites would require tearing down modern areas. This presents obvious problems, and as a result, much of ancient Philadelphia remains lost to history.

Philadelphia means "brotherly love." When King Eumenes II of Pergamum founded the city of Philadelphia, he named it after his younger brother and successor, Attalus II Philadelphus. Attalus II earned the nickname Philadelphus ("one who loves his brother") because of his deep loyalty to his older brother— to the point that when the Romans offered to help Attalus overthrow Eumenes and take the throne, Attalus turned down the offer.[137]

Philadelphia, which sits atop the same fault line as Sardis, was also greatly affected by the severe earthquake in AD 17. Within just a few years of the earthquake, the Greek philosopher and historian Strabo wrote:

> Philadelphia has not even its walls secure, but they are daily shaken and split in some degree. The people continually pay attention to earth-tremors and plan their buildings with this factor in mind.[138]

To the Christians living in this environment, Jesus writes His sixth Revelation letter.

## HOLY AND TRUE

Jesus begins with a dual self-description. First, He presents Himself as God:

> *To the angel of the church in Philadelphia write: These are the words of him who is holy and true... (Revelation 3:7).*

The way this is translated into English, the words *holy* and *true* seem like adjectives. But in the Greek, these words are preceded by the article *the*, making them not just descriptions but titles.[139] In other words, it should read, *"These are the words of him who is the holy and the true...."* Jesus is announcing two of His titles: the Holy One and the True One. These titles are

---

[137] Wilson, *Biblical Turkey*, 295.
[138] Quoted in Fee, *Revelation* 50.
[139] Fee, *Revelation* 51.

significant because they are used throughout the Bible to refer to God the Father. For example, Psalm 22:3 says, *"Yet you are enthroned as the Holy One; you are the one Israel praises."* Later in Revelation, God the Father is referred to as the *"Sovereign Lord, holy and true"* (Rev. 6:10). And Jesus again assumes these titles in Revelation 19:11, where He is called *"Faithful and True."* By taking these titles for Himself, Jesus is reminding the Philadelphians that He is one with God.

## THE KEY OF DAVID AND THE OPEN DOOR

After reminding the believers of His divinity, Jesus expands upon His statement, *"I hold the keys of death and Hades"* (Rev. 1:18), saying:

> *...who holds the key of David. What he opens no one can shut, and what he shuts no one can open. I know your deeds. See, I have placed before you an open door that no one can shut...* (Revelation 3:7–8).

Not only does Jesus hold the keys of death and Hades, meaning that He has overcome them, but He also holds the key of David. In other words, He is the long-awaited son of David who has inaugurated the new covenant Kingdom of God that will never end (see 2 Sam. 7). The key of David is only mentioned specifically in one other place in the Bible, Isaiah 22. There, it is also connected with the ability to open and close doors. The prophecy of Isaiah 22:22 declares: *"I will place on his shoulder the key to the house of David; what he opens no one can shut, and what he shuts no one can open"* (Isa. 22:22). In Isaiah 22, God promises to remove the evil Jewish religious leaders and replace them with a righteous leader. This righteous leader is the one described in verse 22.

As we now know, that prophesied righteous leader is Jesus. This is essentially the picture Jesus paints in Matthew 23–24, where He first reprimands the religious leaders of His day and declares the destruction of the Temple, and then says He is inaugurating the new covenant. The teachers of the Law and the Pharisees, as the defenders of the old covenant, were those who *"shut the door of the kingdom of heaven in people's faces"* (Matt. 23:13). As a result, God was removing them from leadership.

Here in Revelation, Jesus echoes this same picture and promise, but on a smaller scale, to the believers of Philadelphia, who were experiencing great persecution from the Jews. In the midst of this persecution, Jesus declares Himself as the righteous leader of Isaiah 22 who has come to depose the ungodly Jewish leaders who have rejected the new covenant. David Chilton says it this way:

> Christ is thus announcing that the officers of apostate Israel are false stewards: they have been thrown out of office, removed from all rightful authority, and replaced by the One who is holy and true (cf. 1 Pet. 2:25).[140]

The new covenant came at Jesus' death, resurrection, and ascension, yet these leaders were clinging to the old covenant, and because of that, they would experience the judgment of AD 70 that was coming upon the old covenant system and the Temple. Jesus, the one with the key of David, is closing the door on the old covenant and those who cling to it, and He is opening the door for the spread of the new covenant gospel.

---

[140] Chilton, 127.

Other New Testament passages that speak of an "open door" confirm that this phrase often refers to the expansion of the gospel (see John 10:7–9; Acts 14:27; 1 Cor. 16:9; 2 Cor. 2:12; Col. 4:3; Rev. 3:20; 4:1).[141] As N.T. Wright says:

> Jesus is the one who, like the steward appointed over God's house in Isaiah 22.22, has 'the key of David': the royal key that will open, or lock, any and every door. Equipped with this regal power, Jesus has opened a door right in front of the Philadelphia Christians, and he is urging them to go through it. As with Paul's use of the same picture (1 Corinthians 16.9; 2 Corinthians 2.12; Colossians 4.3), the meaning is almost certainly that they have an opportunity not just to stand firm but to make advances, to take the good news of Jesus into places and hearts where it has not yet reached. The qualifications are all in place.[142]

The Jewish leaders of Philadelphia were excommunicating Christians and closing the door of the synagogue against them. In response to this, Jesus tells them, "I am opening My door for you, and no one will be able to close it."[143]

## THE SYNAGOGUE OF SATAN

The next section of the letter continues along the same lines, specifically addressing the Jewish leaders who are persecuting the Christians in Philadelphia:

---

[141] Robertson, 317.
[142] Wright, 34.
[143] Wilson, *Revelation*, 32.

*...I know that you have little strength, yet you have kept my word and have not denied my name. I will make those who are of the synagogue of Satan, who claim to be Jews though they are not, but are liars—I will make them come and fall down at your feet and acknowledge that I have loved you (Revelation 3:8–9).*

> MODERN APPLICATION:
> The new covenant people of God are the true Jews (no matter their ethnicity).

This is the second mention of the synagogue of Satan in the seven letters (the first was in the letter to Smyrna), and once again it is in reference to the Jews who were persecuting the Christians. This means the Jewish presence in Philadelphia must have been significant, and considering how close Philadelphia is to Sardis, with its very large Jewish population, this is no surprise. What is surprising is that archeologists have not been able to locate any remains of an ancient synagogue in Philadelphia.[144] The only evidence they have found is an inscription saying a synagogue of the Hebrews existed there.

These Jews, like the ones in Smyrna, *"claim to be Jews though they are not, but are liars"* (Rev. 3:9). This, once again, is a reference to the reality of Romans 2—that what matters in being Jewish is not physical circumcision but circumcision of the heart. Thus, the new covenant people of God are the true Jews (no matter their ethnicity), and the false Jews are those who cling to the old covenant. This battle between the old covenant false Jews and the new covenant Christians is mentioned again and again in the New Testament. It was one of the main struggles of the early Church leading up to AD 70.

---

[144] This may be, in part, because of the difficulties in excavating the ancient city, since the modern city was built directly atop it.

It is also one of the clearest proofs that these letters were written before AD 70. When the Roman army came through these cities to squelch the Jewish revolt, they were on a mission to kill every Jew they could find. Because of this, after AD 70 the Jewish people had no power and little ability to persecute the early Church. As a people group, they had been utterly devastated. Persecution from the Jews only makes sense if these letters (and the Book of Revelation as a whole) were written before AD 70.

N.T. Wright describes the dynamics of the pre–AD 70 world of this letter:

> There was almost certainly a significant Jewish community in Philadelphia; Sardis, not far away, was a major Jewish centre at the time. As in the letter to Smyrna, we have here an indication that the synagogue community was using its civic status to block the advance of the message about Israel's Messiah, Jesus, a message so very Jewish and yet so challenging to Jewish people. We should not imagine a 'church' on one street corner and a 'synagogue' on another, as in many cities today. We should imagine a Jewish community of several thousand, with its own buildings and community life, and a church of probably two or three dozen at most, holding on to the highly improbable, and extremely risky, claim that the God of Israel had raised Jesus from the dead. That imbalance goes some way to help us explain what is now being said.[145]

---

[145] Wright, 34.

Because of this imbalance, the Jews were able to use their significantly greater numbers and their influence to make life very hard for the Christians in their city. Although we don't know for sure which city in Asia Minor they were from, we read of Jews stirring up a crowd against Paul in Acts 21:27, which shows the ongoing difficulty of the early church at the time. We don't know the specifics of what this looked like for Philadelphia, but we know it must have been difficult, because Jesus points out that they had *"little strength."* They were worn and battered, yet they had remained faithful to Him.

As a result, Jesus promises, *"...I will make them come and fall down at your feet and acknowledge that I have loved you."* This is a reference to Isaiah 60:14, which says, *"The children of your oppressors will come bowing before you; all who despise you will bow down at your feet...."* Originally, God made this promise to the nation of Israel as they experienced persecution from their gentile neighbors. Now, He takes that promise and applies it to His new covenant chosen people. Not only will the false Jews bow down at the feet of the Christians, repenting for their persecutions, but they will also acknowledge that God loves the Christian believers. This is significant, because the Jews viewed the Christians as heretics. Jesus is promising that these Jews in Philadelphia would eventually realize (like the apostle Paul) the covenant shift that had taken place and that they had been fighting against the true people of God.

Some of those who persecuted them would eventually be won for the gospel. This is, perhaps, the open door Jesus mentions, as Milton Terry points out:

Here some of that synagogue are made to come and worship along with the faithful servants of him who has the key of David. This shows further what a door is opened at Philadelphia, and how Satanic foes are made to come through it and acknowledge and worship Jesus Christ as Lord. Those who thus *come and worship* meet the condition imposed in Matt. xxiii, 39, Eph. ii, 19-22; 1 Cor. iii, 16.[146]

This is a great promise for the Christians in the midst of persecution. Not only will Jesus vindicate them, but He will bring some of their persecutors to repentance and to the new covenant. This is one of the greatest rewards persecuted believers could ask for—that those who had harmed them would see the powerful fruit of the Kingdom in their lives and, as a result, turn to Christ.

## THE HOUR OF TRIAL

Next, Jesus promises the persecuted believers safety from the coming destruction:

> *Since you have kept my command to endure patiently, I will also keep you from the hour of trial that is going to come on the whole world to test the inhabitants of the earth. I am coming soon. Hold on to what you have, so that no one will take your crown* (Revelation 3:10–11).

In our English translations, Jesus' statements about the coming "hour of trial" sound very global. It's coming upon the *"whole world"* and *"the earth."* The problem is, the statement begins with a specific promise to *"you"*—to the Christians at Philadelphia in the first century. It does not make sense to push

---

[146] Terry, 308–309.

the fulfillment of this promise several thousand years in the future. It would be completely irrelevant, then, to the people who first received it. And, the modern city of Alaşehir has almost no Christian presence. It just does not make sense to interpret this promise on a worldwide scale.[147] Instead, we must find an interpretation that would have been relevant to the first century recipients of the letter. It was, after all, written to them, not us.

This is further substantiated by Jesus' statement, *"I am coming soon"* (Rev. 3:11). When He said this, He meant *soon*, not two thousand or more years in the future. If we interpret this statement to apply to any time period other than the first century, we distort Jesus' words and actually reverse the meaning of *soon* to *a long time from now*. The logical answer is that when Jesus said He was coming soon, He was referring to the soon judgment on Jerusalem in AD 70. This coming was very relevant to His first century readers, because they were suffering at the hands of the Jewish leaders. Their suffering would end after the judgment, because the Jews would no longer have the strength to persecute them. And in the midst of the destruction, Jesus would keep the believers at Philadelphia safe. This is what Jesus promises them.

In light of that clear time frame, we must understand Jesus' statement about *"the hour of trial that is going to come on the whole world to test the inhabitants of the earth."* The problem with our understanding of this statement is that the English translations have mistranslated several key words. The way this verse reads in English sounds very dramatic and global, but to get that meaning in the Greek, John would have needed to use the word *kosmos*, which means "the whole planet."[148] Instead, he used two words that indicate a local, specific context.

---

[147] Eckhardt, 39.
[148] *Strong's Concordance*, Greek #2889.

First, the word translated as *"the whole world"* is, in the Greek, *oikoumenēs*. It means "the inhabited earth," "the inhabitants of the earth," and "earth."[149] It is, as John A.T. Robinson says, "not the physical earth, but the world of men as explained by the next clause."[150] Likewise, the word translated as "earth" is the Greek word *gēs*, which means "a local area or tract of land."[151] The definitions of these words have a clearly local, small scale meaning, not a global one. David Chilton points out that this phrase *"the inhabitants of the earth,"* or *"those who dwell on the earth"* (NKJV), is used "twelve times in Revelation (once for each of the twelve tribes) to refer to apostate Israel (3:10; 6:10; 8:13; 11:10[twice]; 13:8, 12, 14[twice]; 14:6; 17:2, 8)."[152] Clearly, it is meant to refer specifically to the Jews of the first century. They are the ones who dwell in the land, the localized context of the great tribulation.

Into this context, Jesus declares, *"I am coming soon. Hold on to what you have, so that no one will take your crown"* (Rev. 3:11). This is very similar to the promise Jesus makes to the other church that was experiencing great persecution—Smyrna: *"Be faithful, even to the point of death, and I will give you life as your victor's crown"* (Rev. 2:10). In both instances, the crown is a reward for persecuted Christians who persevere and stay faithful to Christ. Both Paul and James also refer to the crown believers will receive. Paul says this *"crown of righteousness"* is awarded *"to all who have longed for his* [Christ's] *appearing"* (2 Tim. 4:8). In other words, he specifically links it to the period leading up to the AD 70 destruction, when the old covenant was removed and the new covenant fully established.

---

[149] *Strong's Concordance*, Greek #3625.
[150] Robinson, 319.
[151] *Strong's Concordance*, Greek #1093.
[152] Chilton, 129.

James speaks of the crown of life as a reward for faithfulness in the midst of persecution:

*Blessed is the one who perseveres under trial because, having stood the test, that person will receive the crown of life that the Lord has promised to those who love him* (James 1:12).

This crown should not be seen as a royal crown (though we are sons and daughters of the King) but as a victor's crown, "the wreath given the victor in the games."[153] We see this meaning clearly in Paul's comparison of the Christian life to an Olympic competition: *"Everyone who competes in the games goes into strict training. They do it to get a crown that will not last, but we do it to get a crown that will last forever"* (1 Cor. 9:25; see also 2 Tim. 2:5). This victor's crown awaited the believers who remained faithful to Christ during the tribulation events of the first century.

## A PILLAR IN THE TEMPLE

After reminding the Philadelphian believers to hold onto their crown, Jesus closes His letter with two Messianic promises. The first promise is: *"The one who is victorious I will make a pillar in the temple of my God. Never again will they leave it..."* (Rev. 3:12). To understand the significance of the pillars, we must first determine what temple Jesus means here. The Temple in Jerusalem, which God had abandoned, was destined for destruction, and the spiritual new Jerusalem does not contain a

---

[153] Fee, *Revelation*, 55.

physical temple (see Rev. 21:22).[154] Instead, Jesus speaks to them about the spiritual temple.

Based on imagery from the rest of the New Testament, we can see that the new covenant temple is the body of believers, the Church. This is most apparent in Ephesians 2, where Paul uses the metaphor of God's house to describe the Church. Believers are *"members of his household, built on the foundation of the apostles and prophets, with Christ Jesus himself as the chief cornerstone"* (Eph. 2:19–20). Each believer is part of the whole. In other passages, Paul uses the picture of a body (see 1 Cor. 12:27; Eph. 4:11–15; Col. 1:24) to refer to the Church; here he uses the metaphor of a temple:

> *In him the whole building is joined together and rises to become a holy temple in the Lord. And in him you too are being built together to become a dwelling in which God lives by his Spirit* (Ephesians 2:21–22).

Like a body, a temple is a glorious whole built of many unique and necessary parts. In First Corinthians 3, where Paul addresses disunity in the Church, he uses this image to remind the believers of their need of one another. When they are together, God's Spirit lives in their midst. Together—not on their own—they are the temple of God:

> *Don't you know that you yourselves are God's temple and that God's Spirit dwells in your midst? ...God's temple is sacred, and you together are that temple* (1 Corinthians 3:16–17).

---

[154] Robertson, 319; Fee, *Revelation*, 55.

N.T. Wright agrees with this assessment:

The first Christians, partly because of Jesus and partly because of the gift of the spirit, regarded themselves as the true Temple, the place where the living God had made his home.[155]

Peter also uses this imagery to describe the believers being built together to form God's house:

*As you come to him, the living Stone—rejected by humans but chosen by God and precious to him—you also, like living stones, are being built into a spiritual house to be a holy priesthood, offering spiritual sacrifices acceptable to God through Jesus Christ* (1 Peter 2:4–5).

God's temple is not a physical temple, like the one in Jerusalem or like the pagan temples that dotted the acropolis; rather, it is made up of the people of God. Knowing that the temple of God refers to the unified Church, we can see that its pillars (like the foundation Paul mentions in Ephesians 2:20) are its leaders. In fact, Paul uses this exact word to refer to several of the apostles, calling them *"those esteemed as pillars"* (Gal. 2:9). From this, we can see that being called a *pillar* implies being a strong leader within the Church.

This pillar imagery becomes even more meaningful when we remember that Philadelphia was known for earthquakes strong enough to collapse temples. Because of the region's many earthquakes, temples in Asia Minor were often built with earthquakes in mind. After digging out the foundation for a new

---

[155] Wright, 33.

temple, the builders would first lay down a layer of charcoal. Atop that they put wool fleeces and then the foundation stones, clamped together with metal brackets. This design gave the foundation fluidity and enabled it to move without collapsing the temple. When the earth would shake, the temple would float on top of this moving base. This meant "the temples would be among the most secure structures in the city."[156]

If the temple was seen as a secure structure, the pillars and the foundation of the temple were what made it so. The image of pillars has "metaphorical and personal use, with a double significance of being firmly fixed and giving stability to the building."[157] The foundation beneath the ground made the temple earthquake proof, and the pillars held the above ground architecture in place. Thus, to the Philadelphians, the pillars of a temple would have symbolized not only leadership but also stability and strength. A pillar is something that stands strong and firm and is able to endure, even when the earth shakes, because of its foundation. This is a picture of the Church and its leaders. Jesus' promise to the believers at Philadelphia is that, if they endure, He will make them into strong leaders in His Church. He will make them into those who can stabilize and strengthen the whole.

# A NEW NAME

Second, Jesus promises:

> *...I will write on them the name of my God and the name of the city of my God, the new Jerusalem, which is coming*

---

[156] Wilson, *Revelation*, 33.
[157] Robertson, 319.

*down out of heaven from my God; and I will also write on them my new name. Whoever has ears, let them hear what the Spirit says to the churches* (Revelation 3:12–13).

This promise builds upon the first, giving us the image of pillars with names written on them, which was actually a common practice in that area in the first century.[158] As pillars in the temple of God, the overcoming Philadelphian believers would have three names written on them—the name of God, the name of the New Jerusalem, and the Lord's new name.

This promise of a new name and a new city also related to the recent history of Philadelphia. When the earthquake of AD 17 had destroyed much of the city, Rome had loaned them the money to rebuild.[159] To honor the Roman emperor at the time, Tiberius, for his generosity, they had actually renamed the city Neocaesarea.

Later, in AD 69, when another earthquake destroyed the city and Rome sent more money, Philadelphia renamed itself Flavis in honor of the emperor Vespasian.[160] This earthquake and rebuilding happened after the writing of this letter from Jesus to Philadelphia. Thus, not only did Jesus' promise of a new city and new name speak to their recent past, but it would also become an anchor and encouragement in their near future, when they again were destroyed and rebuilt.

In the space of fifty-two years, Philadelphia was twice devastated by an earthquake. Many of the Christians would have lived through the first earthquake of AD 17, and nearly

---

[158] Wilson, *Revelation*, 33–34.
[159] Sardis was wealthy enough to rebuild their own city, so they refused Roman assistance, but Philadelphia accepted the money.
[160] Wilson, *Revelation*, 297.

all of them would experience the coming earthquake in AD 69. Into this environment of instability and loss, Jesus declares that He has a new city and a new name. He has a temple that can never be shaken, and His followers are pillars of stability and strength. All of this points to the new covenant realities of Christ's Kingdom.[161] To this, David Chilton adds:

> All this speaks of the full restoration of God's people to the image of God, as we see in the final chapter of Revelation: "And they shall see His face, and His shall be in their foreheads" (Rev. 22:4).[162]

This promise was one that would have been especially meaningful to the believers in Philadelphia as they faced the trials in their near future. It was a pledge of both belonging and stability.

Though their earthly city had experienced and would experience great upheaval and change, the Kingdom of God would never be shaken (see Heb. 12:28). Philadelphia was renamed more than once after its patrons, the emperors who claimed to be gods and demanded worship in the Imperial Cult. Unlike these fickle and often cruel emperors, the eternally good God promised to write His name on His followers. "The writing of Christ's name on their foreheads is the ultimate sign of ownership, but an ownership not of enslavement but of ultimate and glorious freedom."[163] They would be forever marked as part of His family, as pillars in His house.

---

[161] *"The new Jerusalem (tes kaines Ierousalem).* Not *neas* (young), but *kaines* (fresh). See also 21:2, 10 and already Gal. 4:26 and Heb. 12:22." Robertson, 320.
[162] Chilton, 131.
[163] Fee, *Revelation,* 56.

Of course, this writing of names also foreshadows several later events in Revelation. First, in Revelation 13 the beast writes his name on the foreheads and right hands of his followers. Those who do not accept the mark of the beast, we can assume, have God's name written on them instead (like these Philadelphian Christians). Second, in Revelation 19:11–21, Christ the heavenly warrior forever defeats the beast. Afterward, He is given the new name *"King of kings and Lord of lords."* "Now in anticipation of that scene the victors in Philadelphia are promised to have that name written on them as well."[164]

This is the amazing picture we get of the church in Philadelphia. Though they were experiencing tremendous persecution, Jesus promises that judgment will soon come upon the Jews who are persecuting them. In light of this, the believers are encouraged to persevere just a little longer. Judgment is knocking at the door. When it comes, the false Jews will see the truth, and some will turn to Christ. Through it all, Christ will strengthen them as unshakable pillars and call them His own. This letter of encouragement, from beginning to end, is exactly what the believers in Philadelphia needed.

---

[164] Ibid.

# ten

# LAODICEA–VOMITVILLE

Laodicea, the seventh city to receive a Revelation letter from Jesus, was named after Laodice, the wife of Antiochus II, the founder of the city. Laodicea was one of three cities nestled together in that region—Laodicea, Hierapolis, and Colossae. It was built along the river Lycus and rose 564 feet above the nearby plains.[165] Today, it is uninhabited, and excavation of the ruins has unearthed many structures and artifacts dating back as far as 4000 BC.

In the first century, Laodicea was the banking capitol of ancient Asia Minor, which meant it was very wealthy. "It was the home of the millionaires. There were, of course, theatres, a stadium, and a gymnasium equipped with baths. It was a city of bankers and finance."[166] In fact, Laodicea was so wealthy that, like Sardis, it declined Roman aide after the city was partially destroyed by an earthquake in AD 61.

---

[165] Mills, 79.
[166] Hendriksen, 76.

It was a proud thing to do. Most would have jumped at the offer. But Laodicea reckoned it didn't need outside help. It was quite rich enough, thank you very much.[167]

Because Laodicea was the regional banking capitol, it was also a major trade route crossroads where people from Syria, Ephesus, Europe, and the Mediterranean gathered to do business. During that time in history, Laodicea was especially known for three things—their black wool, their medicinal eye salve, and their lukewarm water. In the first century, Laodicea was home to approximately 100,000 people, which was a sizeable city for that time. In fact, it was the last major population center on the route through Asia Minor toward Jerusalem. When Vespasian first took the Roman army to besiege Jerusalem, he traveled along this route. And later, when Titus came with two legions of Roman soldiers, on his way to the conflict that would result in the AD 70 destruction of Jerusalem, he also passed through Laodicea.[168]

Though the Bible does not mention the apostle Paul visiting Laodicea, we know he had relationship with some of the believers there and wrote at least one letter to them. This letter is lost to history, except for a reference to it in Paul's letter to their neighbors at Colossae: *"After this letter has been read to you, see that it is also read in the church of the Laodiceans and that you in turn read the letter from Laodicea"* (Col. 4:16). To this same church, which had become complacent in its wealth, Jesus addresses His final Revelation letter, warning them of what was coming.

---

[167] Wright, 37.
[168] Mills, 79.

## RULER OF CREATION

First, Jesus introduces Himself, saying: *"To the angel of the church in Laodicea write: These are the words of the Amen, the faithful and true witness, the ruler of God's creation"* (Rev. 3:14). Here He gives three descriptions of Himself—the amen, the faithful and true witness, and the ruler of creation.

In modern Christianity, *amen* is generally understood to mean "so be it," but David Chilton points out that its meaning is actually much more forceful. "It is really an oath: to say amen means to call down upon oneself the curses of the Covenant (cf. Num. 5:21–22; Duet. 27:15–26; Neh. 5:12–13)."[169] This relates to both the old covenant and the new covenant. Jesus, as the Amen, is coming in judgment against Jerusalem, the Temple, and the old covenant. He is, as John Eckhardt says, "the one throughout the Revelation who witnesses against the broken covenant and executes the curses of the covenant."[170]

But Jesus is also the Amen of the new covenant, the guarantee of the covenantal promises. Through His life, death, and resurrection, He has established the new covenant, and all of God's promises are fulfilled in Him. The apostle Paul uses this same terminology when discussing God's promises in Christ: *"For no matter how many promises God has made, they are 'Yes' in Christ. And so through him the 'Amen' is spoken by us to the glory of God"* (2 Cor. 1:20). This is the fullest meaning of amen in the new covenant. Through Christ, the weight of the old covenant was removed, and the new covenant was established.

---

[169] Chilton, 133.
[170] Eckhardt, 47.

Thus, our amen in liturgical response to God's word is both an oath and a recognition that our salvation is wholly dependent not upon our keeping of the Covenant but on the perfect covenant keeping of Jesus Christ, who placed Himself under the Covenant stipulations and curses in our place.[171]

In this statement, then, Jesus warns the Laodicean believers of His coming in judgment against the old covenant and reminds them that He alone has established the new covenant. It is not because of their own righteousness that they are able to have relationship with God. This is important because, as we will soon discover, the believers at Laodicea have become self-satisfied and self-sufficient. They need a reminder of their need for Christ.

Jesus also calls Himself the "faithful and true witness," declaring that He is "the One whose eyes not only see exactly what is going on in the hearts of these people of Laodicea but whose lips also declare the exact truth as seen."[172] According to the Old Testament law, a matter was judged by the testimony of two or three witnesses (see Deut. 17:6). This practice was also affirmed by Jesus and Paul (see Matt. 18:16; 2 Cor. 13:1). Here, Jesus presents Himself as the most faithful witness, the one so perfect He could be the *amen* to the new covenant. His witness, He declares, stands on its own. This is exactly the argument He made when the Pharisees accused Him of appearing as His own witness:

*Even if I testify on my own behalf, my testimony is valid, for I know where I came from and where I am going....*

---

[171] Chilton, 133.
[172] Hendriksen, 77.

*In your own Law it is written that the testimony of two witnesses is true. I am one who testifies for myself; my other witness is the Father, who sent me* (John 8:14, 17–18).

This is affirmed again later in John's vision: *"I saw heaven standing open and there before me was a white horse, whose rider is called Faithful and True. With justice he judges and wages war"* (Rev. 19:11). Jesus is the Faithful and True, the one whose witness stands all on its own. As the faithful and true witness, Jesus is coming in judgment on the old covenant. But before He does, He is warning His complacent followers, telling them, like the believers at Sardis, to get ready.

Lastly, Jesus describes Himself as the ruler of creation. This speaks to His victory over the devil, who had taken the authority over creation from Adam and Eve in the Garden. In His death and resurrection, Jesus took back the authority over the earth (see Matt. 28:18). Now He is the ruler of God's creation. As such, He spends the remainder of the letter communicating in naturalistic terms—gold, eye salve, and water. Using these natural elements, He points to the deficit in the believers at Laodicea.

## NEITHER HOT NOR COLD

Jesus begins by comparing the temperature of their water to their spiritual lives:

> *I know your deeds, that you are neither cold nor hot. I wish you were either one or the other! So, because you are lukewarm—neither hot nor cold—I am about to spit you out of my mouth* (Revelation 3:15–16).

Without understanding the historical context, many Christians have interpreted this passage to mean that hot is an "on-fire, emotionally passionate" Christian and cold is an unbeliever. This is incorrect. The whole thrust of this passage hinges on the fact that Laodicea had a very real water problem. The city was built along the river Lycus, but it often dried up, and as a result, Laodicea had to look to its two neighbors—Hierapolis and Colossae—for a consistent water supply.[173]

Hierapolis was famous for its hot mineral springs, and people would travel from all over to bathe in them in hopes of healing for skin diseases and joint pain. To this day, tourists travel to visit the hot springs of Hierapolis, where the mineral-filled water bubbles out of the ground and pours over a cliff, creating what looks like a snow-covered mountain but is really hardened white mineral deposits. In search of a water supply, Laodicea built aqueducts to carry this water the five miles from Hierapolis to Laodicea. N.T. Wright describes the success of this endeavor:

> But by the time the water arrived in Laodicea it was no longer hot. It was merely lukewarm. What was worse, the concentrated chemicals made it unsuitable to drink, unless for medicinal reasons you wanted to make yourself physically sick.[174]

Further, because of how many mineral deposits were in the water, the terra cotta piping system would very quickly fill with minerals and become so encrusted that the water couldn't get through any more. To combat this, they invented an ancient

---

[173] Wright, 37–38; Wilson, *Revelation*, 34.
[174] Wright, 37–38.

version of manhole covers that opened to allow them to clean the sections of piping. This build-up in the piping caused a serious problem on top of their lack of a good water supply.

While Hierapolis was famous for hot water, Colossae was famous for cold water. It was near the snow-capped Mount Cadmus, and from its heights flowed quick-moving and very cold streams of clear water. However, as that water traveled the aqueducts to Laodicea, eleven miles away, it became lukewarm because of the usual Turkish heat.[175]

Laodicea had a real water dilemma. Whether they looked to Hieropolis or Colossae, their water was lukewarm. David Chilton summarizes the problem this way:

At Colossae, one could be refreshed with clean, cold, invigorating drinking water; at Hieropolis, one could be healed by bathing in its hot, mineral-laden pools. But at Laodicea, the waters were neither hot (for health) nor cold (for drinking).[176]

Thus, Jesus' wish that they were *either hot or cold*" is a comparison to the hot waters of Heirapolis and the cold waters of Colossae. Both were useful, but the lukewarm water at Laodicea was good for nothing—especially in a climate where temperatures regularly exceeded 100 degrees Fahrenheit. In such hot weather, the hot baths and the cool drinking water both presented a wonderful contrast, but lukewarm water was disgusting. It was the kind of water one would be tempted to spit out. This threat to spit the Laodiceans from His mouth

---

[175] Wright, 37–38; Wilson, *Revelation*, 34.
[176] Chilton, 134.

refers back to the Book of Leviticus, where God warns Israel, *"If you defile the land, it will vomit you out as it vomited out the nations that were before you"* (Lev. 18:28). This vomiting is directly connected to idolatry; it is a curse that comes from walking away from God in pursuit of other gods.

This is what Jesus is alluding to with the Laodiceans. He is saying, "I am going to have to vomit you out of My mouth because of how much you have walked away from Me." Spiritually, they are facing a real crisis. In this regard, the church at Laodicea is similar to the church at Sardis. Both appeared to be thriving, but on the inside they were spiritually dead. They were not contending in spiritual battle, and because of it, they faced no persecution. Instead, they were lulled into comfort by their riches. They had allowed themselves to become like the lukewarm water, with its putrid mineral smell, that characterized their city in the natural. So Jesus uses this natural example to tell them, "Spiritually, you taste like the gross water in your city; I wish, instead, you were a cool and refreshing drink or a hot and healing bath."

Sometimes, preachers will use this passage to suggest that it would be better to be "spiritually cold" like an atheist than to be a lukewarm Christian. That is absolute nonsense. God would much rather a person be a lukewarm Christian than an atheist, because He would prefer a little bit of relationship over no relationship at all. Yes, He does not want His followers to remain lukewarm, but He would prefer that over them walking away altogether. Such an interpretation of this passage does not make sense and gives us a distorted view of God. The truth is, in this metaphor, both the hot and cold water were good. Both were presented as a positive contrast to the good-for-nothing spirituality of Laodicea.

David Chilton gives an insightful explanation of what Jesus' critique of Laodicea really means:

> The basic accusation against Laodicea is that it is ineffectual, good for nothing. The Laodicean church brings neither a cure for the illness nor a drink to soothe dry lips and parched throats. The sort of Christianity represented by Laodicea is worthless. The church provided "neither refreshment for the spiritually weary, nor healing for the spiritually sick. It was totally ineffective, and thus distasteful to its Lord." Thus, says Mounce, "the church is not being called to task for its spiritual temperature but for the barrenness of its works." This explains Christ's statement: I would that you were cold or hot. He is not saying that outright apostasy is preferable to middle-of-the-roadism; rather, He is wishing that Laodicean Christians would have an influence upon their society.[177]

The problem with their complacency is that they are making no impact for the gospel, and that is not OK with Jesus. Jesus wanted His Church to be powerfully demonstrating the gospel and winning as many people to Him as possible. In particular, He wanted as many Jews as possible to be saved from the coming destruction. The believers at Laodicea were not living up to this call.

---

[177] Chilton, 134.

## POOR, BLIND, AND NAKED

After using the local water situation to paint a vivid picture of Laodicea's lack, Jesus then points to their three greatest assets in the natural as signs, once again, of their need:

> You say, "I am rich; I have acquired wealth and do not need a thing." But you do not realize that you are wretched, pitiful, poor, blind and naked. I counsel you to buy from me gold refined in the fire, so you can become rich; and white clothes to wear, so you can cover your shameful nakedness; and salve to put on your eyes, so you can see. Those whom I love I rebuke and discipline. So be earnest and repent (Revelation 3:17–19).

Here, the things Jesus rebukes them for were the things they were most well-known for in the natural. Though Laodicea was the gold and banking capital of the region, He tells them, "You are poor; you need to buy gold from Me so you can become truly rich." Telling a poor person to "buy gold" seems almost like a cruel joke, except that the first century listener would have connected this statement to the similar statement made by the prophet Isaiah:

> Come, all you who are thirsty, come to the waters; and you who have no money, come, buy and eat! Come, buy wine and milk without money and without cost. Why spend money on what is not bread, and your labor on what does not satisfy? Listen, listen to me, and eat what is good, and you will delight in the richest of fare. Give ear and come to me; listen, that you may live. I will make an everlasting covenant with you, my faithful love promised to David (Isaiah 55:1–3).

Although Revelation 3:17 doesn't explicitly mention what it means to be "truly rich," Isaiah 55:3-5 tells us of the new covenant, the everlasting covenant:

> *Give ear and come to me; listen, that you may live. I will make an everlasting covenant with you, my faithful love promised to David. See, I have made him a witness to the peoples, a ruler and commander of the peoples. Surely you will summon nations you know not, and nations you do not know will come running to you, because of the Lord your God, the Holy One of Israel, for he has endowed you with splendor* (Isaiah 55:3-5).

Here, Isaiah says God will give several things. He will give an everlasting covenant, He will love with the same love He has for David, He will make us rulers with authority, and the nations will come running to us because we have God and His splendor. This is what Jesus alludes to when He offers the Laodicean believers "true riches."

Laodicea was also known for its black wool. The local shepherds had developed a special breed of black sheep that had very fine and high quality wool. The clothing made from this wool was very popular.[178] However, Jesus tells them, "You are naked; you need to buy white clothing from Me to cover your shameful nakedness." In contrast to their black wool, Jesus offers them His white garments. This admonition to buy white clothing parallels Jesus' letter to the other wealthy and complacent church, Sardis, where He promises that the faithful believers will wear white garments (see Rev. 3:4).

---

[178] Wright, 37–38.

Last but not least, Laodicea was also known as the home of Phrygian Powder. This special powder, when mixed with the mineral-laden water from Heirapolis, created an eye salve that Laodicean doctors had been famous for since the days of Aristotle.[179] In fact, the medical school of Laodicea specialized in ophthalmology, the healing of the eyes. People would travel great distances to get this eye ointment in hopes of healing their eyes.[180] However, Jesus tells them, "You are blind; you need to buy My eye salve so that you can truly see."

MODERN APPLICATION:
Sometimes God uses the natural things in our lives as an illustration to speak to us about our spiritual lives. He says, "In the natural you really have this going on, but in the spirit you also need to have it."

Jesus addresses every area in which the people of Laodicea had become smug and proud. They thought they did not need a thing, but they were wrong. When Rome had offered them financial assistance, they had proudly turned it down. It seems they had adopted the same attitude spiritually. Now Jesus calls their bluff. He tells them the true state of their hearts, which are poor, naked, and blind. In the natural, the believers had it all together. They had the gold, the clothing, and the eye salve, but they were missing it spiritually. Using creation to speak to them about their true condition, their desperate spiritual lack, Jesus tells them (like Sardis) that they actually need a wake-up call. They need to repent.

To repent, they do not need to get rid of their natural assets—their gold, fine clothing, and eye salve. That is not what He is saying. Instead, He's pointing out that these natural things

179 Chilton, 136.
180 Wright, 37–38.

mean nothing if the believers do not also have the spiritual counterparts. His desire is that they would have both, that their natural wealth would fuel their spiritual growth, not detract from it.

## KNOCKING AT THE DOOR

After this stern rebuke, Jesus reminds the Laodicean Christians that His goal is relationship with them: *"Here I am! I stand at the door and knock. If anyone hears my voice and opens the door, I will come in and eat with that person, and they with me"* (Rev. 3:20). He is not going to force them to repent, but He invites them to turn back to Him. That is the kind of King He is.

Many modern preachers use this picture of Jesus knocking at the door as a salvation invitation, saying that Jesus is knocking at the doors of people's hearts. While it is true that Jesus knocks at the hearts of those who do not yet know Him, that is not the meaning of this passage in context. Here, Jesus is addressing people who were already Christians, and He is showing them His heart toward them, even as He rebukes their actions.

To do this, He employs an image His hearers would have easily understood. In that day, when a Roman centurion or ruler arrived at the gate of a city, he would forcefully demand entrance, pounding on the door and saying, "Behold, I am here! Open the gates!" Those inside were required to immediately open the doors and feed the visiting dignitary. The Romans did this in a negative, over-lording, and intimidating fashion. But as is implied in Matthew 5:38–42, where Jesus told the Jews how they should respond to the unfair demands of Roman soldiers, it was common (and it still is) for those in authority to abuse their power.

In contrast to that aggressive and demanding leadership, Jesus gently knocks on the door and asks for entrance. He asks to be welcomed in so that He can share a meal with His followers. By using the word *if,* Jesus implies that opening the door is optional. The Christians at Laodicea have a choice. They do not have to open the door and let Him in. They do not have to repent and heed His warnings. But if they do, He will share a family meal with them. Jesus is, after all, the servant-hearted and humble king, and He demonstrates that to His followers even as He rebukes them for becoming complacent. Though He is the ruler of creation, He does not demand entrance or abuse His power. He does not demand a banquet served to Him by His servants; He requests a meal with His friends. He comes humbly and gently knocks. This is the heart of God on display toward His children, even the ones who have wandered from Him.

We may also see this, as N.T. Wright suggests, as an image of "the bridegroom, knocking on the door of the house where his beloved lies asleep."[181] The people of God are, after all, called the Bride of Christ (see Rev. 21:2). The believers at Laodicea are in danger of falling asleep spiritually, but Jesus their Bridegroom is knocking at the door, calling, *"Open to me, my sister, my darling..."* (Song of Sol. 5:2). He woos them with His kindness because, as Romans 2:4 says, *"God's kindness is intended to lead you to repentance."* This is the thrust of this passage: In it, Jesus demonstrates the type of King He is and the type of heart He carries.

---

[181] Wright, 40–41.

## SITTING ON HIS THRONE

Finally, Jesus ends His letter with this Messianic promise to the faithful believers:

> *To the one who is victorious, I will give the right to sit with me on my throne, just as I was victorious and sat down with my Father on his throne. Whoever has ears, let them hear what the Spirit says to the churches* (Revelation 3:21–22).

In ancient Israel, co-regencies, where the king shared his throne with his son or his mother, were common (see 1 Kings 2:19; 2 King 21:2). In a similar fashion, Jesus promises to share His eternal throne with His followers.[182] Jesus foreshadowed this glorious reality when He equated His followers with His family, saying, *"Whoever does the will of my Father in heaven is my brother and sister and mother"* (Matt. 12:50). The new covenant Kingdom is a family, and each member is adopted as a child of God and a co-heir with Christ (see Rom. 8:17; Eph. 1:5). Through His death and resurrection, Jesus became *"the firstborn among many brothers and sisters"* (Rom. 8:29). In a beautiful and counter-cultural provision, *"Both the one who makes people holy and those who are made holy are of the same family. So Jesus is not ashamed to call them brothers and sisters"* (Heb. 2:11). Believers, as Christ's siblings, are invited to sit with Him and reign with Him on His throne.

This is the current new covenant reality for all faithful followers of Christ—not far off in the future at the end of the world, but right now. As Paul declares, *"Those who receive God's*

---

[182] Wilson, 36.

*abundant provision of grace and of the gift of righteousness reign in life through the one man, Jesus Christ"* (Rom. 5:17). David Chilton shows that the believer's reign with Christ is a current reality:

> But Christ has entered upon His Kingdom already (Col. 1:13); He has disarmed Satan and the demons already (Col. 2:15); and we are kings and priests with Him already (Rev. 1:6); and just as He conquered, so are we to go forth, conquering in His name. He reigns now (Acts 2:29–36), above all creation (Eph. 1:20–22), with all power in heaven and earth (Matt. 28:18–20), and is engaged now in putting all enemies under His feet (1 Cor. 15:25), until His kingdom becomes a great mountain, filling the whole earth (Dan. 2:35, 45).[183]

The believers in the first century were looking forward to the full establishment of the new covenant Kingdom through the destruction of the old covenant in AD 70. In light of this, Jesus is telling them, "I am about to fully come into My Kingdom, and I want you to sit with Me on My throne." He invites them to partner with Him in establishing His Kingdom on earth. Though they had been spiritually lukewarm and ineffective up till this point, they have the potential to reign with Christ.

Looking at history, we can see how this was walked out in the city of Laodicea. In the first century, the Temple of Zeus, which was also an Imperial Cult temple, was the most prominent landmark in Laodicea. Its huge structure demonstrated the priority and influence of the pagan religions at that time. By contrast, the church in Laodicea was meeting in houses (see

---

[183] Chilton, 139.

Col. 4:15). This was a period of great persecution—from both the Jews and Nero—for most Christians in the world at that time. Yet after AD 70, the persecution of the Church began to diminish, and the Church rose up to contend with the forces of paganism and imperialism. Eventually, Christianity was legalized by Constantine's Edict of Milan in AD 313, the persecution stopped, and the Church began to take over the pagan temples. In Laodicea, the former Temple of Zeus was turned into a church in the fourth century. In total, archeologists have found the ruins of twenty-three church buildings in Laodicea. As Christianity grew and paganism diminished, each of the pagan temples was taken over by the Christians and reutilized as churches.

Some people look back at history and think Christians adopted or compromised with paganism, but the opposite happened. The idea of the paganization of Christianity is a Protestant myth that is unsubstantiated by history. Instead, paganism was overwhelmed and defeated by the growing Church. That is why Christians took over the pagan temples, not because they were embracing syncretism but because they were eradicating idol worship so thoroughly that the temples were no longer needed. So the Christians took these old, beautiful buildings, destroyed the statues and idols, and repurposed them as Christian churches. They took the pagan holidays, which were celebrated throughout the Roman Empire, and they changed them to be about Jesus. This was a good thing. It doesn't represent compromise but Christianity influencing and changing culture, even to the point of changing the meaning of major holidays.

Really, the Christians stole the position and influence of the pagan religious system of their day, and they took what was once pagan and made it the Kingdom of God. This is significant when we think about how intertwined the Roman government and culture were with pagan idolatry. What Jesus, through His Church, accomplished in the years following AD 70 was a major cultural upheaval. In Laodicea, for example, when the true ruler of creation, Jesus, set up His throne, He began to take the place of the various pagan deities who claimed to be gods or goddesses of various natural elements. They pretended to be rulers of creation—until the real ruler showed up and His Kingdom began to expand and overtake their kingdoms.

The same happened with Judiasm. Prior to AD 70, the Jews dominated and persecuted the Christians. But as the Kingdom of God expanded, Christianity took the lead as the carriers of God's gospel for the whole world. In Laodicea, an ancient pillar, which may have been part of a synagogue, vividly shows the way the Church grew to dominate. This pillar has an image of two Jewish symbols—a menorah and a shofar. Carved atop these symbols is a Christian cross, showing that Christians took over this formerly Jewish building. As Christianity grew, Judaism declined and was supplanted. The true people of God rose up out of the old covenant Judaism into the new covenant Church (see Rom. 11).

This is the nature of God's Kingdom. In Matthew 13:31–32, Jesus says the Kingdom is like the smallest mustard seed that turns into the largest bush and then turns into a mighty tree that fills the whole garden. Likewise, He compares the Kingdom of God to a small amount of yeast that is mixed through sixty pounds of dough (see Matt. 13:33). That is the nature of the Kingdom. No matter how small it starts out, it is designed to expand and grow until it fills the earth.

> MODERN APPLICATION:
> The Kingdom of God, by nature, is always expanding and growing.

# eleven

# THE HINGE: BEFORE AND AFTER AD 70

Now that we've looked at the individual letters and their historical context, it's important to understand the significance of their structure and how even it communicates meaning. When we read the Bible, most of us do not think about the structure or form of the writing. We are very used to reading prose that does not have a particular form to it. However, for most of history, poetry was the major form of writing. This included spiritual and historical texts, not just what we think of as poetry today.

Thus, much of the Bible, in its original language, is written in a form of Hebrew poetry called the Chiastic Arch or Hebrew Ring Composition. This structure is used throughout the Bible, but many of us have not noticed it simply because we are unfamiliar with the form. It is one of the primary ways poetry is written in Hebrew, and it lends a specific emphasis to the text that often draws out subtle meanings.

The Chiastic Arch follows this pattern:

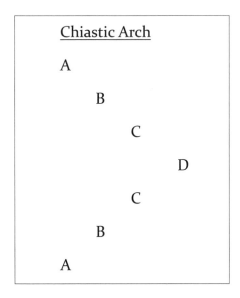

Instead of dividing the verses or ideas in a linear fashion, as we typically do in English, many Hebrew poems follow this cyclical arch form in which the first three parts (A, B, C) progress together toward a central idea (D). The final three parts (C, B, A) progress together back toward the original idea, bringing the poem full circle. Some chiasms are longer, and some are shorter, but the basic form stays the same regardless of length. The text is split in half, with the central idea being the longest and most important. The corresponding parts (A and A), while not usually identical, are similar and often help to explain each other. This pattern of repetition brings clarification and emphasis to the meaning of the poem.

Once we understand and recognize Chiastic Arches, the nuances of this form bring added depth and meaning to passages. The entire Book of Revelation is itself in the form of a Chiastic Arch, as well as the seven letters in Revelation 2–3.

# CHIASM IN REVELATION

Before we look at how the Chiastic Arch features in the seven letters of Revelation, we will first look at the Chiastic Arch present in the entire Book of Revelation:

A – Greeting

    B – Seven Churches

        C – Seven Seals

            D – Seven Trumpets, Angel, Two Witnesses

                E – Woman, Dragon, Male Child

            D – Two Beasts, Angel, Seven Bowls

        C – Destruction of Babylon

    B – Bride

A – Epilogue

At the beginning and end (A) are the greeting and the epilogue. The first B is the seven churches, and the second is the New Jerusalem and the Bride. Both of these are the Church, but there is a progression that happens from the state of the seven churches in part one to the Bride of Christ, who surfaces in part two after the marriage supper of the Lamb. We will look at this in more depth later. The first C is the seven seals, and the second is the destruction of Babylon. The D on the first side is the seven trumpets, an angel, and the two witnesses. Then, the D on the other side is the two beasts, an angel, and the seven bowls. The parallelism of this structure is striking. In the middle (E)—the central event—we find the woman, the dragon, and the male child.

This central event (in Revelation 12) is the most important point, the centerpiece of the book.[184] It is the story of the incarnation. The woman is a picture of the remnant of Israel (the true followers of God),[185] and she gives birth to a male child who *"will rule all the nations with an iron scepter"* (Rev. 12:5; see Ps. 2:9). This child is the covenant promised child—Jesus. The red dragon who is at war with the child and with Michael the archangel is the accuser of the brethren, Satan. When he is defeated and cast out of Heaven, he begins to fight against the woman's other children. These children who come after the firstborn, Jesus, are the early Christians, the true Israel.

In Revelation 12, we get the whole picture of the gospel and the story of the formation and finalization of the new covenant. Jesus comes to earth as a child and defeats the devil through His life, death, and resurrection. Because of this, the devil begins to fight against the early Church, which is the great persecution they faced in the years leading up to AD 70. This is the great centerpiece and turning point of Revelation. Everything in the first half of the book leads toward it, and everything in the second half leads from it and is informed by it.[186]

---

[184] It is commonly accepted that Revelation is a Chiastic Arch. The only debate is over how to divide it up. Mark Wilson's *The Seven Victor Sayings of Revelation* covers the different versions of a Chiastic Arch in Revelation. In most cases, commentators agree that chapter 12 is the centerpiece.

[185] Some say the woman is Mary, the mother of Jesus, because she literally birthed Jesus; however, this is a prophetic picture of the group or movement that birthed the Messiah into the world. That group is the faithful remnant of Old Testament Israel.

[186] If futurists and historicists understood Chiastic Arch structure, they would be forced to abandon their systems of interpretation. Both of these systems are predicated upon the idea that Revelation is written in sequential order, but this is not so. Even the fact that Revelation 12 returns to before the birth of Christ clearly throws the idea of the book being sequential to the wayside.

## THE BEFORE AND AFTER

The turning point of the events of the book can be demonstrated by the *before* and the *after*. Everything hinges on the Lamb's opening of the scroll in Revelation 5, which is the beginning of the judgment events that destroy the old covenant and fully establish the new covenant. These events begin with the opening of the seals on the scroll (the first C) and culminate with the destruction of Jerusalem (figuratively Babylon[187]) (the second C). In the middle, in Revelation 12, is the cosmic summary of the spiritual significance of the AD 70 events—the end of the old covenant and the full installation of the new. Thus, we could say that all of Revelation hinges on the *before* and *after* of AD 70. That one event, which is the focus of Revelation, was a turning point in the history of the Church. It is second only to the death, resurrection, and ascension of Christ.

Recognizing this brings important clarity to our reading of the Book of Revelation. In the introduction, Jesus tells John, *"Write, therefore, what you have seen, what is now and what will take place later"* (Rev. 1:19). In this verse we see the progression of *before, now,* and *after.* Understanding this is crucial to understanding the book as a whole. The *before* (*"what you have seen"*) is the vision of Jesus on the beach at Patmos and the self-description He spoke to John. The *now* (*"what is now"*) is John's present-tense communication to the seven churches. He writes to them in the present tense because this is his and their current reality (pre-AD 70). The remainder of Revelation is a prophecy regarding the *after* (*"what will take place later"*).

---

[187] If a historicist can see that Revelation 4–11 is about Jerusalem, as many historicists do admit, then they cannot escape the outcome of the Chiastic prose, which determines that the second half of the arch is in direct relation to the first half of the arch.

In Revelation 4, John is taken to Heaven in a vision, where he witnesses a cosmic worship service involving the twenty-four elders and four living creatures. Then, in chapter 5, he sees a scroll *"with writing on both sides and sealed with seven seals"* (Rev. 5:1). When John discovers that no one in Heaven or earth is worthy to break the seals and open the scroll, he weeps. However, one of the elders tells him, *"Do not weep! See, the Lion of the tribe of Judah, the Root of David, has triumphed. He is able to open the scroll and its seven seals"* (Rev. 5:5). This Lamb, Jesus Christ, takes the scroll. This is the seminal moment when the judgments of God against the old covenant are about to be released, and all of Heaven sings a new song in worship of the Lamb.

Kenneth Gentry, one of the greatest living scholars on this topic, points out that the scroll, which has writing on the inside and outside and is sealed with seven seals, looked like a first century divorce certificate.[188] John and the early believers would have recognized it as such. In other words, the scroll was God's divorce certificate to the Great Whore of Babylon (Israel of the old covenant). This picture of a divine divorce between God and Israel is mentioned several times in the Old Testament, when Israel walked away from God (see Isa. 50:1; Jer. 3:8). Here, God makes that divorce final. In this, God was not divorcing Himself from a group of people but from the old covenant. He then steps into the new covenant with both Jews and gentiles.

What we must understand, as we read this, is that when John is taken up to Heaven in Revelation 4, he sees God the Father, but Jesus is not mentioned. John is experiencing prophetically what it was like *before* Jesus arrived back in Heaven as the victor.

---

[188] Gentry, *Navigating the Book of Revelation*, 45–71.

Then, in Revelation 5:1–4, we find this scene:

> *Then I saw in the right hand of him who sat on the throne a scroll with writing on both sides and sealed with seven seals. And I saw a mighty angel proclaiming in a loud voice, "Who is worthy to break the seals and open the scroll?" But no one in heaven or on earth or under the earth could open the scroll or even look inside it. I wept and wept because no one was found who was worthy to open the scroll or look inside.*

When John weeps at the unopened scroll, it is a heart-rending moment—a picture of Heaven without a victorious Jesus. It is difficult to even comprehend such a place. This is the *before*. Thankfully, John continues:

> *Then one of the elders said to me, "Do not weep! See, the Lion of the tribe of Judah, the Root of David, has triumphed. He is able to open the scroll and its seven seals." Then I saw a Lamb, looking as if it had been slain, standing at the center of the throne, encircled by the four living creatures and the elders. The Lamb had seven horns and seven eyes, which are the seven spirits of God sent out into all the earth (Revelation 5:5–6).*

Now, John experiences what it is like to see Jesus unveiled as the victor who can open the scroll, end the old covenant, and forever establish the new covenant. This is the *after*. Revelation 4 is part of John's prophetic vision, but it first shows what *was* before showing *what is to come*. When Jesus the slain Lamb takes the scroll and begins to open the seals, He is systematically removing the old covenant and establishing the new. This is what the first century Church was looking forward to—the end of the old covenant age. This event changed history and our reality as Christians in ways many of us have not understood.

For example, if we do not understand the significance of the *before* and *after*, we will see the worship service of Revelation 4 as our current reality. We will think we should imitate the twenty-four elders and throw our crowns down at God's feet. However, the elders were doing this in the picture of what it was like *before* Jesus was revealed as the Lamb who was slain. Their reality before Jesus arrived on the scene is not our current reality. We know this is true because, in His letters to the seven churches, Jesus promises to give victor's crowns to His faithful followers, and He tells them not to let anyone take their crowns from them (see Rev. 2:10; 3:11). Jesus also promises authority and rulership to His followers (see Rev. 2:26–27; 3:21). These promises would be fulfilled through His coming in judgment in AD 70, as spelled out in the remainder of Revelation.

This means these promises to the faithful believers in Revelation are not future for us; they are available to us right now, because we live on the other side of AD 70. Unlike the twenty-four elders, we are not required to cast our crowns at the feet of Jesus. Instead, He invites us to sit on His throne and to rule the nations with Him. When He took the scroll and opened its seals, ending the old covenant, He made us *"a kingdom and priests to serve our God,"* those who *"will reign on the earth"* (Rev. 5:10). This is our identity in God's new covenant Kingdom. He does not give us crowns so that we can throw them down. He gives us crowns so that we can rule alongside Him as His Bride.

Some people find this idea scary, but the reality is that AD 70 changed things. It was the culmination of the events that began with Jesus' death, resurrection, and ascension. It was the final page in the chapter of the old covenant. This is the central theme of the Book of Revelation, the middle point in the chiasm.

## WHAT *AFTER* LOOKS LIKE

This means that our modern reality is not necessarily the same as that of the Christians prior to AD 70. They lived in the unique forty-year time between the covenants, when the new covenant had been established at the cross, but the old covenant still existed. The whole purpose of Jesus' coming in judgment in AD 70 was to completely remove the old covenant and fully establish the new (see Heb. 8:13). When this happened, the Christian reality changed for the better. On the other side of AD 70, we are not looking forward to Christ's coming and the end of the age. We are not hoping in expectation for the victor promises. Instead, we get to live in the current reality of His promises and the fullness of the new covenant.

We are *now* the Bride of Christ. We are not waiting for the marriage supper of the Lamb. We are already married to Him. However, the New Testament believers were awaiting their marriage to Christ as part of His coming in AD 70. This becomes clear when we look at several statements in the New Testament and the Revelation sequence of events.

In Ephesians 5, when Paul compares earthly marriage to our union with Christ, he refers to the union of Christ and the Church as *"a profound mystery"* (Eph. 5:32). The two are going to become one. However, in Romans 7:1–6, Paul says a woman cannot be married to another man while her first husband is still alive. This would make her an adulterer. Thus, her first husband must die, and then she will be free to marry the new husband. In saying this, he is illustrating what must happen so that the Church can be married, spiritually, to Christ. The first husband is the old covenant, and the new husband is Christ. So, for the Bride to marry Christ, the old covenant first needed to be done away with.

During the first century, the Church lived in the transition period when the first husband was not yet dead. She was betrothed to her new husband, Christ, but not yet married. In other words, there was a forty-year engagement period. This is why, after the Revelation account of the AD 70 events, it then gives an account of the marriage supper of the Lamb. First the old covenant needed to die. Then, the Church could be presented to Christ as His Bride. This is what Paul declared when he wrote, *"Whoever is united with the Lord is one with him in spirit"* (1 Cor. 6:17).

Paul, writing before AD 70, writes as though the marriage has already taken place, as though the Church and Christ have already become one. This is because, in the culture of his day, betrothal was just as binding as marriage.[189] However, the marriage actually happened in the events of Revelation 19. The first mention of the Bride is that she has prepared herself for the marriage: "Let us rejoice and be glad and give him glory! For the wedding of the Lamb has come, and his bride has made herself ready" (Rev. 19:7). This comes after the destruction of Jerusalem

---

[189] "The formal betrothal may take place some years before the marriage. The bridegroom elect sends a present to the girl, the dowry is settled, and if sometime afterwards the engagement be broken off, the young woman, if a Jewess, cannot be married to anyone else without first a paper of divorce from the rabbi." Mackie, 131.

(Babylon) by the beast (the Roman Empire) in Revelation 17.[190] The Roman Empire fought against the Jewish people in AD 70, but they also fought against God by persecuting the early Christians. Thus, as Jerusalem faces its destruction, Jesus calls His followers out from among the Jews: *"'Come out of her, my people,' so that you will not share in her sins, so that you will not receive any of her plagues"* (Rev. 18:4). This describes the historical event when the Christians in Jerusalem fled to Mount Pella, where they were spared from the destruction of AD 70.

After the fall of Jerusalem, the time for the marriage supper had finally come. All this is a picture of the union between Christ and the Church that John wrote about prophetically and that Paul stated beforehand, as though it had already taken place. Then, in conjunction with the destruction of Jerusalem and the end of the old covenant, the new covenant marriage supper took place.[191]

Now, we are on the other side of this marriage supper, and we are the Bride of Christ. The two have become one, and we are equally yoked. We are no longer married to the Law, but we are married to Christ in the new covenant. Because of this, we are now His ambassadors, as co-heirs and co-rulers, to bring

---

[190] For an explanation of why Babylon is symbolic of Jerusalem and the beast is symbolic of the Roman Empire, see Gentry, *Navigating the Book of Revelation*, 141–149.

[191] In Matthew 22:1–7, Jesus says, *"The kingdom of heaven is like a king who prepared a wedding banquet for his son. He sent his servants to those who had been invited to the banquet to tell them to come, but they refused to come. Then he sent some more servants and said, 'Tell those who have been invited that I have prepared my dinner: My oxen and fattened cattle have been butchered, and everything is ready. Come to the wedding banquet.' But they paid no attention and went off— one to his field, another to his business. The rest seized his servants, mistreated them and killed them. The king was enraged. He sent his army and destroyed those murderers and burned their city."* Here, verse 7 connects the wedding of the son with the enraged king bringing justice and burning the city. The AD 70 destruction of Jerusalem and the marriage of the Son are unavoidably connected.

the Kingdom into the earth. We are His Bride, and we live in the new Heaven and new earth, which are the new covenant reality.

As those living on the other side of AD 70, with all the inheritance and all the promises, we get to co-make all things new with Christ (see Rev. 21:5). He has overcome, and through Him, we too have overcome. Understanding this changes how we live. It's not just a revelation that certain events are in our past. It changes our understanding of our identity and purpose on earth.

## CHIASM IN THE SEVEN LETTERS

The experience of the first century Christians is not identical to ours, but we can learn important things from Jesus' letters to them. As with the entire Book of Revelation, the seven letters to the churches are organized as a smaller Chiastic Arch.

A – Ephesus

B – Smyrna

C – Pergamum

D – Thyatira

C – Sardis

B – Philadelphia

A – Laodicea

In accord with this poetic form, the central letter to Thyatira is the longest and most important letter. In it, the main message is against compromise. To those who do not compromise, Jesus promises:

> *I will give authority over the nations—that one "will rule them with an iron scepter and will dash them to pieces like pottery"—just as I have received authority from my Father* (Revelation 2:26–27).

This promise echoes the messianic description of Jesus in Psalm 2 and Revelation 12 (which, like Thyatira, is also the centerpiece of a chiasm). Just as Jesus is the one who *"will rule all the nations with an iron scepter"* (Rev. 12:5), so too, His faithful followers will also rule over the nations, alongside Christ, with an iron scepter. Our co-reigning is a key theme of both Chiastic Arches—both the super-structure arch of Revelation and the smaller arch of the seven letters.

The first three and last three letters, which lead up to and away from the centerpiece, also parallel each other in certain ways. For example, Ephesus and Laodicea, the first and last churches (A), both receive a rebuke for complacency and the threat of losing their church. Jesus threatens to remove Ephesus' lampstand, and He threatens to spit Laodicea from His mouth. Likewise, both of the B churches (Smyrna and Philadelphia) are in the midst of intense persecution and receive a positive commendation from Jesus. The C churches also receive rebukes, but specifically phrased in terms of attack. Jesus warns Pergamum that He will fight against them with the sword of His mouth if they do not repent. And to Sardis, He issues the threat of a midnight attack, like a thief in the night.

Beyond this parallelism, the Chiastic Arch structure points to two ideas that bring greater depth to these letters: a picture of history and the victor sayings.

# A PICTURE OF HISTORY

The first is that the seven letters actually imitate biblical history.[192] Seeing these letters in the light of biblical history adds richness to their new covenant meaning. Here is how the chiasm mirrors biblical history:

A – Ephesus (the Garden)

   B – Smyrna (the Exodus)

      C – Pergamum (the Wilderness)

         D – Thyatira (the Monarchy)

      C – Sardis (the Exile)

   B – Philadelphia (the Rebuilding)

A – Laodicea (the Casting Out)

In Ephesus, Jesus promises, *"To the one who is victorious, I will give the right to eat from the tree of life, which is in the paradise of God"* (Rev. 2:7). This is a picture of the Garden of Eden, where the tree of life stood. In Smyrna, Jesus tells them they will face a ten-day tribulation, followed by victory (see Rev. 2:10). This mirrors the ten plagues, which were followed by the victory of Israel and their exodus from Egypt. Then, in Pergamum, Jesus mentions Balaam and Balak, who enticed the Israelites into sin during their journey through the wilderness (see Rev. 2:14).

---

[192] Chilton, 86–89.

In Thyatira, the centerpiece, the believers are promised authority to rule and a rod of iron, which refer back to King David and the monarchy. The monarchy was the turning point for Israel. It took them from continually building and journeying to a place of identity and stability. It was the Golden Age of Israel, especially under David and Solomon's rule. Thus, Thyatira, the turning point of the arch aligns with the turning point of biblical history. It was the climax of history, and from there on out, Israel digressed.

In Sardis, Jesus addresses those who have a reputation for being alive but are actually spiritually dead. He tells them to repent and awake (see Rev. 3:1–2). This mirrors the period of the exile to Babylon and Assyria in the Old Testament, when only a remnant of the Jews remained faithful to God. Then in Philadelphia, we find the theme of rebuilding, which parallels the next season in biblical history—the rebuilding of Jerusalem under Nehemiah and Ezra. The faithful in Philadelphia are promised a new Jerusalem, just like those who returned from exile were able to rebuild their city.

Lastly, Laodicea is a picture of what is coming for Israel in the first century, when in AD 70 they are literally cast out, or spit out of God's mouth, through the destruction of Jerusalem and the Temple. In His letter to Laodicea, Jesus threatens to spit them out of His mouth if they do not return to Him; this echoes the threat of Leviticus, where God promises the Israelites that if they break their covenant with Him He will vomit them out of the land (see Lev. 18:25, 28; 20:22). The letter to Laodicea, then, in a sense prophesies what is about to happen to the old covenant Israel. In this way, the Chiastic Arch returns full circle to the Garden, where Adam and Eve were cast out for rebelling against God.

In these seven letters, then, we get a picture of the progression of the people of God from the Garden of Eden to the high point of the monarchy under David until they are eventually once again cast out of the land. In this way, this structure demonstrates the completeness of biblical history, from the Garden of Eden to AD 70. It has come to an end, just as it started, and now it is time for something altogether new—the new covenant.

## THE VICTOR SAYINGS

A second way in which the seven letters are part of the Chiastic Arch in Revelation has to do with the seven victor sayings or promises. In the Chiastic Arch that forms the Book of Revelation, the seven letters are the first B, and the Bride of Christ is the second B on the other side of the arch.

A – Greeting

  B – Seven Churches

    C – Seven Seals

      D – Seven Trumpets, Angel, Two Witnesses

        E – Woman, Dragon, Male Child

      D – Two Beasts, Angel, Seven Bowls

    C – Destruction of Babylon

  B – Bride

A – Epilogue

Thus, the Church transitions from its earlier state on the first half of the arch, pre-AD 70, to the fullness of its position as the Bride of Christ on the second half of the arch. We see this in the outworking of these victor sayings. Each of the promises Jesus makes in the seven letters is fulfilled in the Bride of Christ near the end of Revelation.

In the first letter, to Ephesus, Jesus promises *"the right to eat from the tree of life"* (Rev. 2:7). The parallel from the end of Revelation says that the righteous *"have the right to the tree of life"* (Rev. 22:14). So, on one side of the arch is the promise of the right to eat from the tree of life, and on the other side of the arch is the fulfillment of that promise.

This is significant and meaningful for us today, because it shows the progression that happened from *before* AD 70 to *after* AD 70. Before, the believers were promised certain things; after AD 70, the believers received the experience of these promises as the Bride of Christ. After the complete and final victory of AD 70, all believers are now able to eat from the tree of life. We are not waiting for this promise or any of the other promises of these letters to be fulfilled. This pattern is repeated in the remaining six letters. As mentioned previously, though the promises are addressed to specific churches, they are meant for all the faithful believers of the first century. Now, in the years since AD 70, their fulfillment applies to all believers.

To Smyrna, Jesus promises resurrection. They do not need to fear the second death (see Rev. 2:10–11). On the other side of the arch, Revelation 20:6 tells us about the fulfillment of this promise in the first resurrection:

*Blessed and holy are those who share in the first resurrection. The second death has no power over them, but they will be priests of God and of Christ and will reign with him for a thousand years.*

Jesus promises to the believers at Pergamum that He will give them the hidden manna and white stones *"with a new name written on it, known only to the one who receives it"* (Rev. 2:17). By the end of Revelation, Christ's name is written on their foreheads (see Rev. 22:4), and they are invited to the wedding supper of the Lamb (see Rev. 19:9). They are brought into this private feast (which the white stones gave them access to).

In Thyatira, Jesus promises authority over the nations (see Rev. 2:26–27). Then, in Revelation 20:4, there are *"thrones on which were seated those who had been given authority to judge."* Because of their faithfulness to Christ, they are given the authority to rule with Christ and judge the nations. Jesus also promises the believers at Thyatira the morning star (see Rev. 2:28). At the other end of the arch, Jesus reveals Himself as *"the bright Morning Star"* (Rev. 22:16). He is the fulfillment of the promise, which is a promise of Himself and the authority to rule with Him.

To Sardis, Jesus promises to give them clean, white clothing and guarantees that their names will never be blotted from the book of life (see Rev. 3:4–5). At the end of Revelation, we find those who have washed robes (see Rev. 22:14) and *"those whose names are written in the Lamb's book of life"* (Rev. 21:27).

To the church at Philadelphia, Jesus promises to make them pillars in the temple of God and to write on them the names of God, the new Jerusalem (*"which is coming down out of heaven from my God"*), and Christ (see Rev. 3:12). Near the end of Revelation, God's name is written on His followers (see Rev. 22:4). We see the new Jerusalem, which is the Bride of Christ, descending out of Heaven (see Rev. 21:2, 10), and *"the Lord God Almighty and the Lamb are its temple"* (Rev. 21:22). If God and Christ are the temple of the new covenant, believers are the pillars in the temple. They are hidden with Christ in God, as Colossians 3:3 says. This is the divine union of the new covenant.

In the old covenant Temple, people came to meet with God, but they could not dwell in Him. The new covenant gives us a different picture. The new Jerusalem is the Bride (the believers in Christ), and in it, the temple is God, and within the temple are pillars, which are the believers. These overlapping pictures of Christ in us and us in Him show the incredible union that new covenant believers are welcomed into.

Finally, in Laodicea the believers are promised *"the right to sit with me on my throne"* (Rev. 3:21). This is fulfilled in Revelation 20:4, where the martyrs are given thrones to sit on and rule the nations with Christ. In this way, each of the promises from the seven letters finds fulfillment before the end of Revelation.

As mentioned earlier, a picture of the entire story of the new covenant transition is laid out in the central chapter of Revelation 12, which is the center of the chiasm. It leads from the promises *before* to the fulfillment of the promises *after*. As the early Church looked ahead to the coming destruction, the Book of Revelation (which was originally a letter to them) reassured them of the promises and their soon coming fulfillment on the other side of the Great Tribulation, when Israel would be vomited from the land. As they faced a terrible and traumatic time, Jesus used these letters to reassure them of their safety in

God's heart and of victory on the other side. For us, looking back at that time in history, we can be confident that what the early Church looked forward to is now ours in fullness. We are not struggling to be victorious; we start from the place of victory. Because of what is behind us, historically and spiritually, we have inherited all of Christ's promises by faith. This is one of the most important modern applications that we can glean from the seven letters of Revelation.

# CONCLUSION

After reading about the original meaning of the seven letters to the seven churches in Revelation, the natural question for modern readers is: *If this doesn't have a future interpretation, what does it mean for us today?* Some might feel tempted to just throw out the letters. After all, they were isolated to a very unique period of history. Others, who perhaps saw these letters as having futuristic prophetic relevance, may feel as though they have lost part of their framework for how they understood their life and faith.

Neither option is right. Certainly, we never want to discard any part of Scripture as unimportant. For example, the gospels tell a story about a unique time in history, and much of what Jesus said looked forward to His death and resurrection, events that are in our past. Yet, His experiences and sayings are still an important and relevant part of our faith. Though they are in the past, they help us understand our identity as new covenant

Christians. Similarly, beginning to read these letters within their historical context may cause one to lose some bad theology, but in reality, this is positive for one's faith. Proper understanding is the first step toward knowing how to apply the Bible to our modern lives. The fact that these letters were specific to a time in our past, not our future, does not make them irrelevant to our present and future lives.

Within each of the seven chapters about the seven letters, we briefly highlighted several modern application points related to the details of each letter. And in chapter 11, we examined the *before* and *after* of AD 70 and how our modern existence differs from that of the early believers. This is the most important lesson of the Revelation letters. We do not need to struggle to overcome, in hopes of receiving the promises. Because the early believers were faithful and overcame, we get to live in the fruit of their victory. We are not orphans hoping to be adopted. We have been adopted, and all the blessings of Christ are available to us in this life. This is our current reality in the new covenant.

# BIBLIOGRAPHY

Aune, David. *Revelation: Word Biblical Commentary*, vol. 52a. Dallas, TX: Word Inc, 1997.

Beasley-Murray, G.R. *The Book of Revelation*. Grand Rapids, MI: William B. Eerdmans Publishing Co., 1981.

Chilton, David. *The Days of Vengeance*. Dallas, GA: Dominion Press, 1987.

Cimok, Faith. *A Guide to the Seven Churches*. Istanbul, Turkey: A Turizm Yayinlari, 2013.

Eckhardt, John. *Behold I Come Quickly*. Chicago, IL: Crusaders Ministries, 2008.

Eusebius. *The Church History*. Grand Rapids, MI: Kregel Publications, 1999. Translated by Paul L. Maier.

Fee, Gordon D. and Douglas Stuart. *How to Read the Bible for All It's Worth*. 3rd edition. Grand Rapids, MI: Zondervan, 2003.

------. *Revelation*. Eugene, OR: Cascade Books, 2011.

Gentry, Jr., Kenneth L. *Before Jerusalem Fell: Dating the Book of Revelation*. Fountain Inn, SC: Victorious Hope Publishing, 2010.

------. *Navigating the Book of Revelation: Special Studies on Important Issues*. Fountain Inn, SC: GoodBirth Ministries, 2010.

Gregg, Steve. *Revelation, Four Views: A Parallel Commentary.* Nashville, TN: Thomas Nelson, 1997.

Hemer, Colin J. *The Letters to the Seven Churches of Asia in Their Local Setting.* Grand Rapids, MI: Eerdmans Publishing, 2001.

Hendrikson, William. *More than Conquerors.* Grand Rapids, MI: Baker Books, 1940.

Josephus, Flavius. *Antiquities of the Jews.* In William Whiston, trans. *The Works of Flavius Josephus.* Grand Rapids, MI: Baker Book House, 1984.

Mackie, G.M. *Bible Manners and Customs.* Westwood, NJ: Barbour Books, 1991.

Mills, Jr., Jessie E. *Revelation Survey and Research.* Bradford, PA: International Preterist Association, 2004.

Nee, Watchman. *The Orthodoxy of the Church.* Anaheim, CA: Living Stream Ministry, 1994.

Ramsay, W.M. *The Letters to the Seven Churches.* Peabody, MA: Hendriksen, 1994.

Robertson, Archibald Thomas. *Word Pictures in the New Testament*, vol. 6. Grand Rapids, MI: Baker Books, 1933.

Robinson, John A.T. *Re-dating the New Testament.* Norwich, UK: SCM Press, 2012.

Strong, James. *Strong's Exhaustive Concordance of the Bible.*

Terry, Milton. *Biblical Apocalyptics.* Grand Rapids, MI: Baker Books, 1988.

Viola, Frank. *The Untold Story of the New Testament Church: An Extraordinary Guide to Understanding the New Testament.* Shippensburg, PA: Destiny Image, 2005.

Welton, Jonathan. *Raptureless: An Optimistic Guide to the End of the World*, Rev. ed. including The Art of Revelation. Rochester, NY: Welton Academy, 2013.

------. *Understanding the Whole Bible.* Rochester, NY: Welton Academy, 2015.

Wilson, Mark W. *Biblical Turkey: A Guide to the Christian and Jewish Sites of Asia Minor.* Istanbul: Zero Produksiyon Ltd, 2010.

------. *Charts on the Book of Revelation: Literary, Historical, and Theological Perspectives.* Grand Rapids, MI: Kregel Academic, 2007.

------. *Revelation: Zondervan Illustrated Bible Backgrounds Commentary*, 3rd ed. Grand Rapids, MI: Zondervan, 2010.

------. *The Victor Sayings in the Book of Revelation.* Eugene, OR: Wipf & Stock, 2007.

Wright, N.T. *Revelation for Everyone.* Louisville, KY: Westminster John Knox Press, 2011.

# RECOMMENDED READING

*The Art of Revelation*
DR. JONATHAN WELTON

*Biblical Turkey: A Guide to the Christian and Jewish Sites of Asia Minor*
MARK WILSON

*Charts on the Book of Revelation: Literary, Historical, and Theological Perspectives*
MARK WILSON

*The Days of Vengeance*
DAVID CHILTON

*The Letters to the Seven Churches of Asia in Their Local Setting* COLIN J. HEMER

*Raptureless: An Optimistic Guide to the End of the World*
DR. JONATHAN WELTON

*The Victor Sayings in the Book of Revelation*
MARK WILSON

# WELTON ACADEMY

The Welton Academy Supernatural Bible School Online is neither a supernatural ministry school nor a dusty seminary. We have created a unique program that teaches the depths of the Word without becoming boring or denying the supernatural. We are focused on teaching the Bible through a New Covenant Kingdom perspective.

It is our passion to see all Christians operate in the supernatural, know their identity, walk in freedom, and be powerful people. We are not simply aiming at creating pastors and missionaries. No matter what your calling is, you must have a firm foundation in your identity, freedom, and the supernatural. We think long-term and build powerful people.

To be a part of where the Lord is leading the Church in the years to come, we must lay a new foundation in our understanding of the Word. The Word hasn't changed, but some of our understanding of it must change; otherwise, we will hinder our growth and the advancement of the Kingdom of God.

A powerful advantage of the SBS is that while you are spiritually growing you are not isolated. You have the opportunity to interact with others who are growing in the same deep things you are learning. You are joining a movement with others who are pressing forward with God.

Go to www.weltonacademy.com for registration and more information.

# Additional Material by Dr. Jonathan Welton

# UNDERSTANDING THE WHOLE BIBLE
## The King, The Kingdom, and the New Covenant

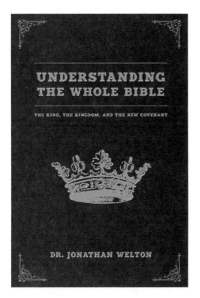

This textbook is the distillation of a nineteen-week course, Understanding the Whole Bible from Genesis to Revelation taught by author and theologian Dr. Jonathan Welton. If you want to devour the Word, this textbook will give you the knife, fork and even tuck in your napkin and teach you how to eat! Topics include: - Learn the difference between Systematic and Biblical Theology - How did we get our Bible? - Translations and study tools - Freewill versus Predestination - Dispensationalism and Covenant Theology - Cessationism and Supernaturalism - The Five Major Covenants: Noah, Abraham, Moses, David, and the New Covenant - The Covenant Promises fulfilled - God is not an Old Covenant monster - Understanding the At-One-Ment - Better Covenant Theology - The Great Covenant Transition - The End of Age - The Unveiling of Jesus - The One Law of the New Covenant World.

What others have said:

*This is an instant classic. 'A book that shows the Bible is the story of God's covenant journey with His people.' Dr. Jonathan Welton has presented one of the most comprehensive and revelatory books on the King, the Kingdom, and the New Covenant.*

*Jonathan Welton has shifted my entire understanding of the Bible and his book provides so much clarity on what the Bible really is saying. Seeing Scripture through the lens of the covenants is so needed and many miss this vital perspective.*

# Additional Material by Dr. Jonathan Welton

## RAPTURELESS
## Third Edition

In 2012, the best-selling author and founder of Welton Academy, after ten years of thorough research, released the first edition of Raptureless. It has gone viral and has sent a shockwave through the Charismatic/Pentecostal church world. Dr. Welton's writing gift has made Raptureless one of the easiest to read yet deepest quality books on the subject of the endtimes. He proves beyond a shadow of a doubt that the Great Tribulation is an event, which occurred in the First Century. Without complicated wording, he demonstrates that the AntiChrist is not a person in our future, and that we are not waiting for Jesus to be enthroned in Jerusalem. Basically, this book is the opposite of everything you thought you knew about the endtimes, simply written and thoroughly, historically proven. Now available in it's third edition, with new editing and chapter reordering, as well as 60% more content than the original.

What others have said:

*"Jonathan Welton has taken a bold step in confronting one of the greatest 'sacred cows' of our day: end time theology! The fear created by the expectation of a coming antichrist and a great tribulation are keeping many believers in bondage. Many believe that defeat is the future destiny of the Church. In his easy to read presentation, Jonathan dismantles many of the popular ideas in the Church about the end times."*     ~ Joe McIntyre

# Normal Christianity: If Jesus is Normal, what is the Church? by Jonathan Welton

Jesus and the Book of Acts are the standard of *Normal Christianity*.

Remember the fad a few years ago when people wore bracelets reminding them, What Would Jesus Do? Christians state that Jesus is the example of how to live, yet this has been limited in many cases to how we view our moral character. When Christians tell me they want to live like Jesus, I like to ask if they have multiplied food, healed the sick, walked on water, raised the dead, paid their taxes with fish money, calmed storms, and so forth. I typically receive bewildered looks, but that is what it is like to live like Jesus!

Perhaps we are ignoring a large portion of what living like Jesus really includes. Many Christians believe they can live like Jesus without ever operating in the supernatural. After reading in the Bible about all the miracles He performed, does that sound right to you? (Excerpt from book)

## What others have said

I believe before Jesus returns there will be two churches. One will be religious, and the other will be normal. This book of Jonathan Welton's will help restore your childlike faith, and you will become normal!

~ **Sid Roth,** Host of It's Supernatural! Television Program

# Eyes of Honor: Training for Purity and Righteousness
by Jonathan Welton

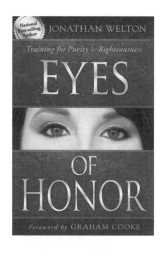

After struggling with sexual temptation for years, author Jonathan Welton devoted himself to finding a way to be completely free from sexual sin. He read books, attended 12-step groups, and participated in counseling—with no success.

Spurred on by countless friends and acquaintances who shared a similar broken struggle and longed for freedom, the author searched Scripture. There he found the answer, which he shares with you in a compassionate, nonjudgmental way.

*Eyes of Honor* helps you understand how to live a life of purity by realizing:

- Your personal identity
- How to view the opposite sex correctly
- Who your enemies are

*Eyes of Honor* is honest and refreshing, offering hope and complete freedom and deliverance from sexual sin. Jesus' sacrifice on the cross and your salvation guarantee rescue from the appetite of sin. Your true identity empowers you to stop agreeing with lies of the enemy that ensnare you.

"This book is stunningly profound. He got my attention and kept it." **~ Dr. John Roddam**, St. Luke's Episcopal

"Jonathan has written one of the best books on being free from bondage by dealing with the root issues of sin. I highly recommend reading this book."

**~ Dr. Che Ahn,** Chancellor Wagner Leadership

# NEW COVENANT LEADERS

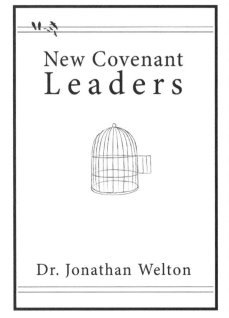

When it comes to leadership books, we find a vast sea of titles. How is this book any different? The answer is simple. This is not a book for those who want a highly controlled environment. This is a book for those longing for the biblical reality of New Covenant-styled leaders. New Covenant leaders are servant-hearted, vulnerable, affectionate, openhearted and transparent. They don't talk about covering or being under spiritual authority, rather they are true mothers and fathers in the faith, and their churches are easily described as spiritual family. Jesus told us leading in the Church looks different than it does in the world. The question is, how? In what ways does it look different? If we ask ourselves, practically speaking, what it looks like to be an equipper, what images come to our minds? Do they involve fame and power or the opportunity to serve? Too often, we in the Church have viewed leadership as more akin to stardom than servanthood. Yet the reality of the role of an equipper-someone who trains others and leads them into maturity-inherently contains the idea of service. Like a good parent, a leader equips his or her followers through service, safety, and affection. These are the marks of the New Covenant Leaders which are emerging in the body of Christ. They do not use their authority to monopolize power and create (often unknowingly) an atmosphere of rules and fear. That is the world's way of leading. Instead, their leadership looks a lot like the way Jesus leads: 1. They exhibit servant-based authority. 2. They create environments where people can be vulnerable and transparent. 3. They are affectionate and warm. In short, they bring healthy family life to church and truly equip disciples instead of indoctrinating followers. In this book, the author examines each of these Jesus-style leadership methods in detail. If you want a revolutionary book on leadership, this is it.

# The School of the Seers by Jonathan Welton

Your how-to guide into the spirit realm!

*The School of the Seers* is more than a compilation of anecdotal stories. It is the how-to guide for seeing into the spirit realm.

The fresh, profound, and new concepts taught in this book take a mystical subject (seers and the spirit realm) and make them relevant for everyday life.This book takes some of the difficult material presented in other seer books and makes it easy to understand, removes the spookiness, and provides practical application of a dimension that is biblically based and scripturally sound. Get ready to enter the world of a seer! In this groundbreaking and revelatory book, Jonathan Welton describes his unique journey in which God opened his spiritual eyes. He shares how you too can activate this gift in your life.

Discover the keys from Scripture that will help you:

- See with your spiritual eyes.
- Use the four keys to greater experiences.
- Recognize what may be hindering your discernment.
- Learn about the four spirits.
- Access divine secrets and steward heavenly revelation.
- Learn how to really worship in Spirit and in Truth.
- Understand meditation, impartation, and so much more...